RENOVATE
INNOVATE

RENOVATE
INNOVATE

RECLAIMED AND UPCYCLED HOMES

ANTONIA EDWARDS

PRESTEL   MUNICH | LONDON | NEW YORK

CONTENTS

INTRODUCTION

Renovate Innovate features a collection of one-of-a-kind dwellings from around the world realized through the innovative reuse of existing structures, materials and objects – a process otherwise known as upcycling. In my previous book *Upcyclist: Reclaimed and Remade Furniture, Lighting and Interiors*, published in 2015, I presented upcycled designs primarily for their aesthetic merits, independent of their association with the environment or thrift. Similarly, in the book you are holding right now, upcycling for residential architecture is observed through the same lens, proving that there is an artistry to reuse and that good design lasts. The designers' motives for each of these projects combine desires to preserve architectural heritage and reap energy-saving benefits or, in some cases, are born out of a necessity for low costs and for convenience. Each design tells a story of how a beautiful and timeless home can emerge out of doing something unpredictable with materials and buildings that others might consider unrecoverable or redundant.

In the dawn of a sharing economy, in which independent homeowners compete with the traditional hotel industry via websites like Airbnb, our curiosity about extraordinary dwellings is growing. With the opportunity to stay in unusual, more personalized, 'lived in' homes now at our fingertips, we are offered rich experiences in places that generic hotel rooms cannot match. Staying in homes rather than hotels opens our eyes to non-commercial, impromptu architectural and interior styles, while increasing our appetite for unique spaces that are a break from the norm.

Another shift that is a sign of the times is the new wave of websites and books fetishizing cabin and tiny house living, indicative of our desire for an escape from urban excess. The charm of these dwellings is that they hint at the simple life, a luxury that many of us crave. Most of the designers in this book have a similarly romantic view towards the homes they have created. The act of stripping things back to the bare essentials and using up what already exists offers respite in a world that is already overwhelmed with too much stuff and too much information. The tiny house movement in particular is suggestive that more of us are realizing the joys of owning less and being in touch with nature. Perhaps for some it also invokes memories of a childhood spent building dens out of whatever materials were on hand.

Reuse may not always be the most straightforward or cost-effective solution. Materials sometimes need to be extracted, cleaned and treated. Old spaces must be stabilized, damp proofed and insulated, all of which can be labour-intensive, expensive work. But as this book demonstrates, those who do take on the challenge can produce homes with an appeal that couldn't be achieved with brand new materials.

This book is divided into three sections: Reclaimed, Revived and Reimagined. Reclaimed features dwellings that have been built using partially or entirely upcycled materials, such as shipping containers, telegraph poles, railway sleepers and even a Boeing 747. Revived features existing residential properties that have been renovated in intelligent ways to highlight the original characteristics of the buildings, in some cases with the application of reclaimed materials and vintage pieces. Reimagined features buildings that used to serve another function and have been converted into living spaces. Examples include a former Methodist chapel, an old chocolate factory, a garden atelier and a cattle barn.

With millions of tonnes of construction waste ending up in landfill each year, common sense dictates that finding ways to divert it is crucial. An adaptable approach and a creative eye, exemplified by the architects, designers and taste-makers in this book, offer a wealth of exciting opportunities and housing possibilities. They are not just utilizing what we've already manufactured and built, but are finding inventive ways to connect the past and the future; the old and the new.

This adaptability is key to home design, because living spaces are extensions of ourselves that inevitably grow and evolve. Relics of the past don't have to be preserved in a time capsule, but can evolve with us. Upcycling and adaptive reuse honour our romantic appreciation for our heritage while respecting the needs of a changing world.

ANTONIA EDWARDS FOUNDER OF UPCYCLIST.CO.UK

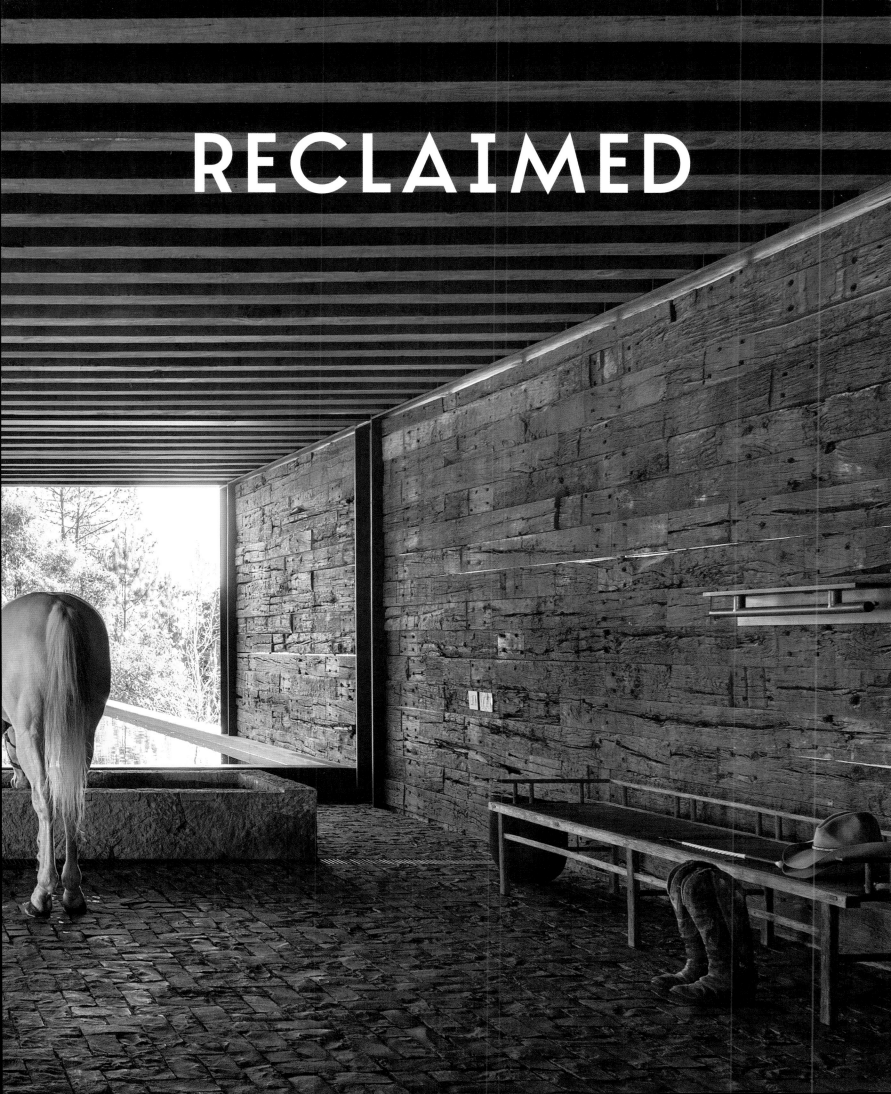

RECLAIMED

ATLANTA TREEHOUSE

PETER BAHOUTH | GEORGIA, UNITED STATES

The secluded Atlanta Treehouse, situated in a quiet location in the heart of Intown Atlanta, has been named Airbnb's most wishlisted property in the world, and guests frequently describe their experience of sleeping there as magical and transformative. The designer behind one of the world's most desirable lodgings is former environmental advocate Peter Bahouth. Bahouth has served as the Executive Director of Greenpeace USA, the Ted Turner Family Foundation and the US Climate Action Network. He is also a stereoscopic photographer. Sixteen years ago he fulfilled his ambition to build three treehouses in the wooded lot next to his house.

The reclaimed materials used to build the treehouses were gathered as Bahouth went along; there were even serendipitous moments of stumbling upon used windows that fitted the exact spaces which needed filling. He found the first treehouse window left out for trash about a block away from his home and replicated it at salvage yards. He also picked up some old, wooden restaurant doors.

He says, 'I didn't want it looking like a prefab and felt it would be a bit contrary to build structures within seven trees that were not respectful of the trees themselves. I think that, when using items made from wood, they should be utilized for longer than the time it took for the tree to produce it.'

Bahouth's interest in one-of-a-kind-ness partly stems from his mother frequently taking him to flea markets as a child. 'I grew up being a collector and preservationist,' he explains. 'I like old, well-crafted things. For me that has always provided some satisfaction; things that don't look like what everybody else has. In Atlanta and in America generally, you can find the same shirt in any city you visit. It's strange how you can be driving down a street that looks just like a street 15,000 miles away. I think people react to that.'

Bahouth believes the popularity of the treehouse is simply down to it offering an experience that's a little bit different. He says, 'We live in a homogenized, pasteurized and franchised kind of world and I think people have a sincere desire to stay in something unique. People know that when they go to a hotel, the rooms above and below them are usually exactly the same. They want to do something special and there aren't many ways to do that.'

Surprisingly, the largest group of guests that come to stay in the treehouse already live in Atlanta, suggesting that visitors are not just looking for accommodation, but are specifically looking to experience Bahouth's magical dwelling. 'I think people like the appeal of being somewhere green in the city and, here, they can almost go camping, with the luxury of a bed,' he posits. 'When I give people the tour, I tell them about the 150-year-old southern shortleaf pine called The Old Man who watches over the place. It gets people to look up, rather than down at their computer.'

RENOVATE **INNOVATE**

RECLAIMED

PHOTOS

page 13 and 14, top right: Bahouth had always wished for a bed on wheels that rolled out onto a platform so you could sleep under the stars. The bedroom of his Atlanta Treehouse also looks out on to a small stream.

page 14, top left: The design for the treehouse was guided by not only the trees, but the collected materials. Some of the reclaimed windows used are about 70 years old and have butterflies pressed between two sheets of glass.

page 14, bottom: The cluster of treehouses is comprised of three separate rooms. They are connected by rope bridges adorned with fairy lights and supported by seven trees, including a 150-year-old southern shortleaf pine referred to as The Old Man.

page 15: Bahouth is an avid collector, so the interior is sensitively furnished with antiques and flea-market finds. The large living-room window was one of the last pieces he sourced and, by sheer chance, fitted the space exactly.

page 16: The living room, otherwise referred to as Mind, contains a small balcony overlooking an acre of woods. The bedroom was named Body and the third tier, Spirit. The latter is a platform that surrounds The Old Man – the largest of the seven trees.

C⊘LLAGE HOUSE

S+PS ARCHITECTS | MAHARASHTRA, INDIA

Shilpa Gore-Shah and Pinkish Shah are founding partners and design principals of award-winning firm S+PS Architects. Both are alumni of the Sir J. J. College of Architecture in Mumbai and the University of New Mexico, Albuquerque.

The concept for their Collage House was based around an ad hoc, eclectic visual language inspired by the found objects and 'collaged' architecture of Mumbai. 'We were very concerned that sustainability in architecture was heavily leaning towards a points-based system, premised on buying products that would achieve so-called "green buildings". Unfortunately, these were dreadful, banal spaces with no soul,' Gore-Shah explains. 'Cameron Sinclair, the co-founder of Architecture for Humanity, once said, "When you build a beautiful building, people love it. And the most sustainable building in the world is the one that's loved." We were interested in exploring an approach that would lead to more delightful and joyous spaces, while demonstrating the use of recycled materials in unexpected ways. These materials carry with them the patina of time, nostalgia and memories of a life lived in another era, none of which are possible to create authentically with the new.'

The collage concept is immediately expressed in the distinctive corner facade of the building, constructed from recycled windows and doors. In and around the house, further reclaimed elements can be found at every turn. Externally, salvaged materials include scrap metal, tile samples, pipe offcuts and stone sourced from the existing site. Inside, flooring is made from old Burmese teak rafters and purlins, while upcycled furniture sits alongside colonial and antique pieces.

'For both of us, having lived in the city of Mumbai for most of our lives, it is impossible to ignore the way half the population lives in informal settlements,' says Shah. 'However, if one looks closely, there are many lessons to be learnt. We were keen to upcycle not only materials but also ideas, knowledge and experience without romanticizing or fetishizing them. We also wanted to explore how these ideas could be made "acceptable" to a more mainstream audience.'

He adds, 'In India, with limited resources, one sees examples of frugality and resourcefulness all around you every day. Nothing ever goes to waste. Everything is infinitely recycled until absolutely nothing more can be done with it. After the economic liberalization of India in the 1990s, with the onset of globalization, one has begun to see the rapid creation and production of waste, especially in urban centres, leading to large landfills. We are unfortunately repeating all the mistakes of the West, in spite of having native methods and systems that can reduce waste. This project attempts to shine light on some of these ideas, but at the same time updates them for the modern age, within the mandate of what architecture can do. We think it is imperative that we deal with this situation of waste holistically. There is a desire for the new and for anything Western in India – unfortunately, sometimes at the cost of erasing valuable local knowledge and native wisdom. Designers will have to continue to find ways to balance these aspirations along with finding new meanings, expressions and value in age-old practices.'

RENOVATE **INNOVATE**

page 19: Collage House is a three-storey home in Navi Mumbai, built for a four-generation family. The striking corner facade is made of windows and doors salvaged from demolished houses in the city. The house is built around a concrete frame, which wraps and connects the spaces from back to front.

page 20, top: The corner facade creates a beautiful interior feature. Coloured and textured glass used in the windows was sourced from Dharavi, one of the largest informal settlements and recycling centres in India. The multicoloured chair is made from chindi, a textile produced from recycled waste fabric.

page 20, bottom, and 21: Metal pipe leftovers sourced from steelyards were pieced together like bamboo to form a 'pipe wall'. Here, rainwater downtake pipes and a sculpture of spouts create a water feature during monsoon season. Hidden below the courtyard is a large rainwater harvesting tank wrapped in rock. The bright, patch-work planter is made from tile samples obtained from ceramic tile vendors.

page 22: A design based on traditional Indian artwork was woven into the wire mesh elevator enclosure.

page 23, top: The doors and windows of the facade were procured from a recycling market in Mumbai called Do Tanki.

page 23, bottom: Stone that was removed from the existing site was used to build walls at ground level.

page 24: In the courtyard, one wall is clad in pieces of rusted scrap-metal plates sourced from shipyards that have been riveted together. Other walls are clad in cut waste stone slivers, rescued from stone-cutting yards and the waste generated onsite.

WHITEHORSE

DESIGNBUILDBLUFF | UTAH, UNITED STATES

The award-winning DesignBuildBLUFF graduate programme, organized by the University of Utah, was started by architect Hank Louis in 2000 in partnership with the Navajo community of Bluff, San Juan County, in the Utah Four Corners region. The Navajo Nation is a reservation belonging to the largest federally recognized Native American tribe in the United States. It covers around 27,000 square miles across Utah, Arizona and northwestern New Mexico.

Louis set up the programme because it not only allows students to be immersed in cross-cultural experiences, but teaches them that design doesn't end with drawings. Working and living onsite, students in the programme receive hands-on training in design and build, while addressing the housing shortage within the Navajo community. In 2013, the programme was taken over by Jose Galarza.

Each year, a group of up to sixteen students are given the opportunity to design and build a full-scale work of architecture for a beneficiary of the Navajo Nation. These are usually small, single-family homes assigned by the local tribal chapters. Working to limited budgets and with an aim to promote sustainability and regenerative design, students are asked to consider alternative building methods while also respecting the social, cultural and environmental needs of the region. The necessity to use appropriate technologies and materials that are available at hand makes salvage an essential component of the designs they create.

The aesthetic for the Whitehorse project was inspired by the vernacular pole barn but also bears a resemblance to a traditional dwelling of the Navajo people known as a hogan. The structure is made up of numerous upcycled elements, with 90 per cent of the exterior reclaimed in some way.

Students reuse all kinds of materials, including wood and steel structures, used windows and doors, telephone poles, train ties, baseball bleachers, salvaged aluminium, mason jars and trinkets, as well as exterior cladding and wood pallets. Old timber becomes stair treads and benches, while a former exterior siding could be re-milled into a trellis. 'Often, materials spark ideas for all kinds of uses in a building, aside from those that are purely structural,' says Galarza. 'Students, partly because of their curiosity and naivety, are able to see new possibilities that a trained person may not.'

Before Galarza became an architect, he co-founded a 're-store' in Western Massachusetts. This was part of a larger initiative that was as concerned with diverting materials from the waste stream as it was with affordability. He explains, 'Given that construction waste is so prevalent in our landfills, it seems crucial that we as designers and manufacturers start to unlearn the concept of waste. The cradle-to-cradle idea is a good example of how designers and material scientists are trying to buck this 20th-century trend. If you look at old timber frames, they last for hundreds of years and even after a long life as a building, they are often repurposed. It seems to me that a truer form of sustainability is the possibility that a building is either safe enough to degrade into the ground as compost, or can be completely repurposed. We can dream, can't we?'

PHOTOS

page 27: Since it is entirely off-grid, the rectangular shape and southern exposure of Whitehorse is designed for optimum passive solar heating.

page 28, top: As the house is raised 4 feet off the ground with recycled telephone poles, the ubiquitous 'blow-sand' passes beneath it rather than quickly piling up alongside it.

page 28, bottom left: Whitehorse is clad in aluminium panelling from a 3Form product press and accented with reconstituted shipping pallets.

page 28, bottom right: Inside, students built a rocket stove that burns kindling-size pieces of wood and heats up the home. Reclaimed lighting, carpets, lockers and shelves were used throughout the interior.

page 29, top: Bluff is located on the San Juan River in the Utah Four Corners Region. The Bluff International Balloon Festival is an annual event.

page 29, bottom: Reclaimed corrugated steel cladding was used on the exterior box. The separate utility shed, which houses the hot-water reservoirs, features a reclaimed wood barn door.

page 30: The air that flows in the shade underneath the house cools and refreshes its back deck. This is an abstracted version of traditional shade structures that are designed for the desert's extreme hot and cold conditions.

747 WING HOUSE

DAVID HERTZ FAIA & THE STUDIO OF ENVIRONMENTAL ARCHITECTURE
| CALIFORNIA, UNITED STATES

David Hertz has been an active participant in environmental and design communities for over three decades. He became a LEED accredited professional in 2004 and, in 2008, was elected to the College of Fellows of the American Institute of Architects. As well as serving on a number of professional committees, he also teaches sustainable design. His own practice, the Studio of Environmental Architecture, based in Venice, California, is devoted to green building and restorative solutions.

747 Wing House is located on a 55-acre property in the remote hills of Malibu, a spectacular location with a unique topography. The client had requested a building with curvilinear feminine shapes. The solution Hertz devised was a floating curved roof that would allow for unobstructed panoramic views across the nearby mountain range, valley and Pacific Ocean, as well as the islands in the distance.

It soon became apparent that an actual aeroplane wing could meet their requirements. After some research, they superimposed different wing types on the site to scale and found that the wings of a 747, at over 2,500 square feet each, offered an ideal configuration that would maximize the views. They would also provide a self-supporting roof, with minimal additional structural support needed.

The 747 was sourced from an aeroplane graveyard in the desert of Southern California. While a new 747 costs at least $250 million, they purchased an intact 1977 model 300 for $35,000, the price of scrap. Large segments of the 747 were reused, including the left and right full wings and the horizontal tail stabilizers. A section of the fuselage, as well as an engine cowling, were also modified into a fountain. 'The scale of a 747 aircraft is enormous – over 230 feet long, 195 feet wide and 63 feet tall with over 17,000 cubic feet of cargo area alone. This represents a tremendous amount of material for a very economical price,' says Hertz.

It took 17 governmental agencies to approve the project. The team contacted the Federal Aviation Administration to register the house on maps so that it wouldn't be confused with a crash site, which even led to a visit from Homeland Security. In addition, five major freeways were closed in order to transport the wings to a local airport where a Chinook helicopter airlifted them to the site. Hertz explains, 'The strategy resulted in a short burst of carbon. However, by minimizing construction, demolition waste and transportation to and from the site, this resulted in carbon savings equivalent to one acre of forest, in comparison to what conventional building would have required.'

He adds, 'Using the wings of a 747 had a profound effect on the final design of the house and informed other ideas, such as using parts of an engine for a fountain. We were inspired by the Native American concept of using every part of the buffalo, which encouraged us to think how far we could push it. Future plans for the site may include utilizing other parts of the airplane's fuselage, making the body into a guesthouse or the nose of the plane into a meditation space.'

Upcycling an aeroplane in this manner is an example of what Hertz defines as 'radical reuse'. He says, 'To melt down an airplane into an aluminium can is a perfect example of downcycling. In this project, making use of one of the most advanced designs in aviation lessened the building's embodied energy while minimizing the use of virgin raw materials. As we continue to use up our primary resources, there is no question we will begin to mine our abandoned and stranded resources as a way to become more efficient; this is a simple reality.'

RECLAIMED

PHOTOS

page 33: The 747 Wing House is nestled in the remote hills of Malibu on a 55-acre property. Five major freeways were closed so that the wings could be transported to a local airport before being airlifted to the site by a Chinook helicopter.

page 34, top: The cockpit windows of the plane were reconstructed into a skylight and the first-class cabin deck was made into the roof of the house. Solar power, radiant heating and natural ventilation are incorporated, as well as high-performance heat mirror glazing.

page 34, bottom: The wings of the 747 were engineered to be strong and light-weight and ended up as ideal materials for the roofs of the house. Frameless, structural self-supporting glass creates the enclosure.

page 35: The idea to upcycle the 747 came about mainly because it offered the precise shape the client was looking for and allowed for optimal views of the stunning landscape by eliminating structure.

page 36: 36: The wing structures are positioned to float on top of simple concrete walls that are cut into the hillsides. The floating roofs derive simple support from steel brace frames. These attach to strategic mounting points on the wing, where the engines were previously mounted. Hertz won an American Architecture Award for work on the 747 Wing House in 2012.

SAIG⊘N HOUSE

The award-winning Saigon House is a four-storey dwelling that was designed for an extended family with five children in Ho Chi Minh City, formerly and still referred to as Saigon. The concept for the building was inspired by a Vietnamese house called Van Duong Phu, also known as Van Duong Palace. The house was built by Vuong Hong Sen, a greatly respected scholar of history and archeology and a famous collector of antiquities, who died in 1996 aged 94. Vuong Hong Sen requested that, upon his death, his house and entire collection of antiquities be donated to the state of Vietnam. He hoped his treasures would be put into a museum that would bear his name, preserving his collection. Sadly, his wishes were not granted. Many of the objects were stolen and the house that was once an architectural masterpiece fell into disrepair for 18 years, eventually becoming a noisy street restaurant.

According to a21studio architect Toan Nghiem, Saigon has transformed beyond recognition, both culturally and architecturally. In honour of Van Duong Palace, a gem of Saigon culture that fell into oblivion, Saigon House was born. Nghiem explains, 'We imagined future generations would only come to know Western-style houses and unemotional streets, sunk deeply into a culture of consumption with little education about the place where they were born and raised. We wanted to make a house inspired by Saigon characteristics, where a family's love and respect for their roots could be passed on to the next generation, in an environment where childhood memories would be cherished.'

He adds, 'Our generation is now familiar with hot and cramped spaces. As a result, they are ready to scramble for every available living space. Our challenge was to make a house that was comfortable, on a popular site of 3 × 15 metres in the city centre, that would be inspired by traditional Saigon elements. We wanted the house to be not only a beloved space for kids, but a living space that would remind adults of their own childhood memories.'

Reclaimed materials were chosen for use throughout the building. Most were collected from demolished houses, including the roof tiles, floor tiles, doors and windows. Nghiem says, 'We were not only interested in the distinctive qualities of aged beauty, we also felt it made a connection between the past and the present. Stories about Saigon live in abandoned things that, in this house, have now come back to life. It would be very easy to talk about the environmental benefits, but it's the story behind the objects that is most interesting. In a material world where everyone buys more than they need and throws things away to buy new, we would like to go another way, that of exchanging things.'

Key design features of the house were inspired by Saigon culture, such as stacking roof layers and rooms open to the courtyard with balconies full of flowers. 'Alleyways are one of the most remarkable features in Saigon, a playground where young children love to play and adults interact with each other positively and respectfully,' Nghiem explains. 'The first time the owners saw the house, they weren't sure about it, but it wasn't long before they fell in love with it. They told me that they now love it so much, they cannot stay in any other place, not even a friend's house.'

page 39: Saigon House is located in a small part of Saigon centre where new and old houses sit side by side. The house is designed to blend into its surroundings, as if it had been there for decades.

page 40 and 41, bottom right: Furniture and materials reclaimed from a bygone era echo the architects' concept of passing on the family's love and appreciation of their home and heritage to the next generation.

page 41, top left: Native trees were planted on the ground floor where the family gathers to eat, as well as on the balconies and steel frames. The large net hanging overhead offers a play area for the children.

page 41, top right: Rays of light shine through the gaps in the flooring directly above, which was also made from reclaimed materials.

page 41, bottom left: Just 3 metres wide, the tall and narrow four-storey house recreates the romantic atmosphere of sunlit Saigon alleyways.

page 42: Every room in the house is modelled on a small dwelling. These structures with sloped roofs sit at different levels, with balconies covered in foliage overlooking a central courtyard, reminiscent of traditional Saigonese architecture. The roof tiles were reclaimed from demolished local houses.

REMISENP∆VILLON

WIRTH ARCHITEKTEN | BREMEN, GERMANY

Wirth Architekten is a Bremen-based office founded by brothers Jan and Benjamin Wirth in 2012. Their approach to architecture aims to give seemingly unimportant rooms – even those with the most tedious or dreary function – a ceremonial atmosphere.

The Remisenpavillon was originally intended to be just a simple garage, but ended up as a multifunctional space. It stands among a group of tall trees and is the first building you see when approaching the adjoining farm, located in Germany's Lower Saxony region. The new structure was designed not to disturb the homogenous ensemble of farm buildings, yet still stand out as an original and independent form. 'The buildings surrounding the Remisenpavillon have no special cornices,' says Jan Wirth. 'They consist of a cube at the ground floor and a nearly 45-degree roof. It became clear to us at a very early stage that the new building had to be made of the same sort of material that was used for the older structures on the site. While we were searching for suitable stones, a burnt-down farm building nearby struck us as the perfect solution.'

The bricks that were salvaged from the ruin were most likely produced over 100 years ago by the same manufacturer as those found on the yard. The bricks could only be extracted by hand, so the client did this himself with the help of friends and neighbours. Once collected, the plaster had to be painstakingly removed, a process that took about a year to finish. Jan explains, 'There aren't many projects where clients, engineers and craftsmen are willing to invest such a tremendous effort. We didn't shy away from using old bricks, even though this meant more work, time and money. We also had to bear in mind the low compressive strength and weakness of the older bricks from frost damage. In that sense, the nature of the used material definitely contributed to the final design. The fact that the new structure merges perfectly into the existing ensemble justifies every effort it took to construct it. Without reusing the brick, that wouldn't have been possible.'

The new pavilion is now used for a variety of functions, depending on the season. It can be utilized as a storage space for firewood and agricultural implements, or for parking cars and tractors. In summer, when the room is empty, it transforms into an office space or garden loggia for receptions and al fresco dining.

Despite the extensive salvage operation behind this particular project, the Wirth brothers think first and foremost that architecture should be based on a good concept and that a singular part, such as the materials, should not be the driving force behind a design. 'It is our belief that the material should subordinate itself to a concept and not the other way round, even if it plays a central part in the final outcome. Design should evolve from the features needed at present, so reusing materials should be considered as an opportune common practice to avoid emotional overcharging,' says Benjamin Wirth. 'When the reclaimed material really fits into the project, however, it can result in an outstanding sensory experience.'

RENOVATE **INNOVATE**

PHOTOS

page 45: From afar the Remisenpavillon looks like a mysterious, closed-up cube. By night, light from recessed fittings set into its ceiling shines through the perforated brickwork, giving the structure a celestial glow.

page 46: The brick structure is now a multifunctional space for storing farming equipment and, in summer, for al fresco dining, parties and other activities.

page 47, top: The broad planks of the gate originate from a colossal old oak tree that had been struck by lightning 15 years previously and was felled by a storm. Local farmers helped to bring it to the nearby sawmill.

page 47, bottom: The masonry has a delicate appearance due to the moulding and special arrangement of bricks, which derives from the subtle brickwork of the late 19th century.

page 48: The unexpected outcome of the Remisenpavillon exemplifies the architects' personal conviction that, by making rooms nice, the activities in them will always turn out to be more enjoyable.

THE LOVE ART STUDIO

KITIPONG NGOWSIRI | PHUKET, THAILAND

Kitipong Ngowsiri was born and raised in Bangkok and holds an MFA in Mixed Media from Silpakorn University. Since graduating with a BFA in Printmaking from Chiang Mai University, Ngowsiri has been making his living as an artist from his studio in Phuket Art Village. A hidden gem of the area, this peaceful creative community in Nai Harn is comprised of studios and galleries that are built by the artists themselves. The creatives that flow in and out of the village are predominantly Thai and regularly come together for exhibitions, workshops and music events.

Ngowsiri's hand-built live/work space, The Love Art Studio, has unsurprisingly become emblematic of the village, as it is constructed from colourful recycled wood sourced from broken boats. The wood was collected over a period of three years and the eye-catching structure continues to evolve. He says, 'Although the timber has changed from a ship into a home, the soul of the ship remains. It has just changed from one state to another. I see beauty in the scars that remain from the wreck, which has come from the vast ocean and has gone through the weathering of time. The Love Art Studio is like bringing together a jigsaw puzzle using my own techniques, a work of art in itself that humans can use on a daily basis.'

The inside of The Love Art Studio is a feast for the eyes: a treasure trove filled with artfully curated and collected objects, figurines and trinkets, set against colourful patchwork walls of reclaimed wood. Ngowsiri uses the space to showcase his own work, but also puts on exhibitions with artist friends from around Southeast Asia, including the Philippines, Myanmar, Malaysia, Indonesia and South Korea.

Every day Ngowsiri gets up early to comb the beaches for objects that get washed up onto the shore. He often incorporates driftwood and other found objects into his own sculpture and installations. 'When we see garbage on the beach or wood from a boat wreck, the natural reaction is to dismiss it as useless,' he explains. 'I see beauty when I pick it up and find stained rust and bright colours. It has a story and value in itself that inspires me to bring new life to it. I also want to spread awareness that people shouldn't dump their garbage into the sea.'

As an adept maker, Ngowsiri creates art in many forms, including sculpture, painting and installation. Themes in his work often reflect on society's state of mind. 'My work tells the story of the events shaping our sensory experience and the importance of time,' he says. 'I urge the viewer to think and feel the shapes of the composition, as well as focus on the beauty of imperfection. I recognize the value of life and I think that art makes us more human.'

PHOTOS

page 51: Situated in Phuket Art Village, The Love Art Studio is constructed from pieces of wood salvaged from broken boats. In total, the process of collecting and building took three years.

page 52, top: Virtually everything in Ngowsiri's house is handmade. The space is personalized with hand-built furniture, whimsical objects and figurines. Vistas through the spaces invite visitors to explore.

page 52, bottom right: The live/work space has rooms for showcasing his own artworks and those by friends from around Southeast Asia.

page 53: Ngowsiri has furnished the wooden studio with a curated collection of sculpture, trinkets and treasures, some of which were found washed up on the local beach.

pages 54–5: The colourful patchwork aesthetic carries through the entire studio, with reclaimed wood details, such as the handmade saloon doors and signposts, appearing around every corner.

CAÑON CITY
CONTAINER CABIN

STUDIO H:T | COLORADO, UNITED STATES

Denver-based Brad Tomecek founded his firm, Tomecek Studio Architecture, in 2013. He sits on the AIA Denver Board of Directors and, in addition to his architectural practice, teaches at the University of Colorado. Tomecek was principal-in-charge for the Cañon City Container Cabin project while with Studio H:T.

Cañon City in southern Colorado is located in a mountain bowl along the Arkansas River. Its unique geography makes it popular with tourists, not only for sightseeing but also sporting activities such as kayaking and rock climbing. The clients for the Container Cabin were a couple who had been visiting the area for years and were looking to create a unique and durable family retreat on hunting land.

'The goal was to build small and off-grid,' says Tomecek. 'Initially we were attracted to shipping containers as a way of re-evaluating how we live and what we live in. Technically, we all live in some sort of box, whether it's stone, wood, drywall or metal. We were interested in understanding the benefits and pitfalls of this type of construction. Uniqueness and reuse also formed part of the clients' personal mantra and so they liked the idea of using shipping containers.'

The cabin is formed of one 40-foot container and six 20-foot containers. These were modified offsite and reinforced for shipping. The master suite is housed in two central containers that form the upper level. These were offset to provide a covered entry to the mountain-facing courtyard, prior to which the structure had to be reinforced at key points, with additional walls built onsite. The two containers that flank the courtyard contain a guest bedroom on one side and a kitchen/living space on the other, with the guest quarters accessed from the exterior deck.

The robustness of the containers makes them resistant to the weather conditions of the exposed location, particularly when the cabin is unoccupied. Facing the Sangre de Cristo mountain range, the decking contains a lowered seating area that provides extra shelter from the seasonal harsh winds and the perfect spot for stargazing. For the wood-lined interior, the clients decided to reuse material from a fallen barn salvaged from their property in Tennessee. The deck railing was also repurposed from another residential project.

Tomecek explains, 'We have learned that the more you modify the containers, the less you can take advantage of their inherent qualities. Reusing materials can yield many different results depending on the goals of the project. You can celebrate the uniqueness of found pieces and express their character, or downplay their individuality to be consistent with the larger whole. We wanted to utilize the containers, because of not only their structure, durability and finish but their unique character. For this reason, we decided to leave the containers exposed rather than try to hide their identity, letting them stand bold and unapologetic.'

RECLAIMED

PHOTOS

page 59: Floor-to-ceiling high-performance glazing at Cañon City Container Cabin offers stunning views of the landscape by day and the starry skies by night.

page 60, top: The seven shipping containers were arranged to create a central courtyard, offering shelter from the harsh seasonal winds.

page 60, bottom: The cabin boasts stunning views towards the Sangre de Cristo mountain range, south of the Rocky Mountains.

page 61, top: The interior has a cosy but contemporary feel, with an industrial staircase and wood-lined walls. The wood was salvaged from a fallen barn on the clients' property in Tennessee.

page 61, bottom: The raw finish of the shipping containers was deliberately kept intact, so as not to hide its identity. A photovoltaic system was put in place for energy and a well with low flow fixtures supplies water to the cabin.

page 62: The sky at night can be enjoyed from the al fresco decking area. The deck railing was repurposed from another residential project.

TELEGRAPH POLE HOUSE

WHBC ARCHITECTS | LANGKAWI, MALAYSIA

Langkawi is a cluster of islands in the Andaman Sea. Situated off the coast of northwest Malaysia, this serene location is known as the Jewel of Kedah and boasts breathtaking white sandy beaches and turquoise seas.

The clients for the Telegraph Pole House were a retired couple who were looking to build a house in the region and were attracted to traditional Malaysian timber longhouses built on stilts. The brief given to Kuala Lumpur-based architects WHBC was to build a house on a small hillock, surrounded by paddy fields, coconut trees and buffalo, in keeping with the traditional craft of the region. With good hard timber running scarce, however, the architects were reluctant. The process would involve cutting down mature trees and painstakingly treating the wood to avoid warping and shrinkage. Keen to find an alternative, they had the idea of repurposing utility poles.

Architect BC Ang says, 'We noticed that timber utility poles were being replaced by concrete columns all over Malaysia not too long ago. These poles are made from beautiful hardwood timber, and have been tested and proven as quality structural timbers. They have been in the elements for decades while maintaining their soundness from impending termite attacks and weathering. They also have a beautiful greyish weathered patina and texture that only time can give to wood.'

WHBC, along with the clients and builders, embarked on the process of sourcing the poles from timberyards in Kedah, Kelantan and Terengganu in the north and east of Malaysia. Having once supported electrical and telephone lines across the country, around 450 poles were reclaimed in total.

The completed house was built around a main structural frame, with roof trusses made from utility poles salvaged from a timberyard in Kedah. Floor and wall boards were reclaimed from a jetty in Penang and the roof shingles were salvaged from an old airport hotel, also in Penang. Contrasting with the wear and patina of the old timber, sleek details such as integrated steel doors, windows, connectors and cables made construction easier and quicker, but also contributed to a more contemporary aesthetic.

The simple layout of the house is open-plan on the ground floor with rooms upstairs. The indoor/outdoor living space at ground level looks out onto a pool area with stunning sea views beyond. Sliding doors provide access to the kitchen, a necessary addition for preventing monkeys and other wildlife from entering.

For WHBC, the Telegraph Pole House is an example of reuse in architecture that goes beyond the environmental. Ang explains, 'We believe the reclamation of material in architecture cannot be solely an altruistic action. It has to be a design solution with very pragmatic reasoning behind it, such as construction, logistics or cost. The practice of reclaiming materials in Malaysia is gaining traction but it is still on a very small scale. It would be great to see if it is possible to explore working with reclamation on a larger industrial level for commercial use or mass housing.'

RENOVATE **INNOVATE**

PHOTOS

page 65: The main beams of the Telegraph Pole House are formed by three tiers of poles. In multiple sections, the beams are connected with scarf joints.

page 66, top: In order to keep as much of the original vegetation surrounding the property as possible, the house is accessed via a steep path rather than a criss-crossing road, which would have meant clearing 2.5 acres of forested land.

page 66, bottom: Telegraph poles were kept in their original state, revealing traces of their previous life. In total, the house was built from around 450 poles.

page 67, top: The house is surrounded by paddy fields and overlooks stunning views of the Andaman Sea.

page 67, bottom: Classic white bedding and textiles contrast with the all-wood interior.

pages 68–9: The space resembles a traditional house on stilts, with bedrooms upstairs and the ground floor open. The kitchen can be sealed off to prevent wildlife from entering.

page 70: The original steel base on the poles prevents termites from attacking the timbers.

HUT ⦶N STILTS

NOZOMI NAKABAYASHI | DORSET, UNITED KINGDOM

Nozomi Nakabayashi's interest in architecture was cultivated simply through observing everyday life. She holds an MArch from the Architectural Association Design and Make programme in Dorset and a BArch from Rice School of Architecture in Houston, Texas. Having grown up in Tokyo and lived in the United States, Nakabayashi is now based in London and has since formed a collective called Torigahappi.

The brief for Hut on Stilts was to create a small and comfortable space high above the ground where the client could spend the night, enjoy the natural surroundings and find inspiration for his writing. The primary structure, which holds the hut high up in the air, is made from reclaimed telegraph poles. Small windows are made from reclaimed glazing fitted with new timber frames. Timber cladding on the walls was also made from offcuts of western red cedar board from a nearby sawmill. The structure was prefabricated offsite, whereas the cladding and interior detailing were completed on location.

During her time in the MArch programme, Nakabayashi developed her building skills while working on a collaborative endeavour called The Big Shed Project. The experience of building the hut herself with just a small team has made working directly and instinctively with materials an important part of her practice. She says, 'Through the programme, I experienced a different kind of designing and making, where you are faced with the physical reality of the materials from the beginning to the end of the project.'

Innovative, eco-friendly materials have been used to insulate the structure. The walls and roof insulation are made of natural cork bonded with resin and the floor is comprised of insulation made from recycled cotton and denim garments. The ceiling is also lined with hessian fabric. Nakabayashi says, 'I was really excited about the beauty of cork insulation at first, the texture, the smell and how it feels, also the idea that it can breathe and insulate at the same time. This initial fascination set a precedent for my preference for using reclaimed and natural building materials in the project. You have to come up with your own way of using the materials and it's a process of testing until it works. This leads you to come up with innovative ways of making things.'

The site conditions were challenging in terms of the building sequence, as there was no power source on site; Nakabayashi chose to build without a generator or scaffolding. 'This meant that all the work was done using battery-powered tools and the roof works were done by harnessing and rope, which required really agile and acrobatic moves at times,' she explains. 'But experiencing the site as I was building, without artificial light, and timing my work with the change of weather and season, was a beautiful experience. Being surrounded by amazing makers, thinkers, foresters and farmers was inspiring and I distinctively sensed a different way of working and living to what I grew up with in the city.'

RENOVATE **INNOVATE**

PHOTOS

page 73: The small writer's retreat Hut on Stilts is elevated by recycled telegraph poles and surrounded by oak trees in the Dorset countryside.

page 74: Eight square metres in size, the cabin has a wood-burning stove, writing desk and bed. The roof and walls are insulated with cork and lined with hessian fabric.

page 75: Nakabayashi's hut was built with the help of a small team using natural, locally sourced and reclaimed materials. The large window was made from recycled glass.

page 76: The bed is contained in a cavity beneath the plywood floorboards and can be covered up when not in use. The window opens out onto a platform offering views of the hills, nearby lake and wildlife.

TINY TEXAS HOUSES

BRAD KITTEL | TEXAS, UNITED STATES

Brad Kittel arrived in Austin, Texas, in 1984 with $640 to his name and the inside of a school bus for a home. He embarked on a career in real estate and spent 12 very successful years renovating and brokering inner-city properties. It led him to regenerate deprived areas of Austin and Gonzales, for which he won awards. After leaving Austin in 1996 to spend time with his young son, he went on to create Discovery Architectural Antiques in Gonzales, selling architectural salvage.

Ten years later, Kittel began constructing Tiny Texas Houses less than 600 square feet in size. He built them with toxin-free salvaged materials, without any need for importing, cutting down trees or creating new glass, sinks, bathtubs or hardware, and for no more money than the cost of human energy. This marked the first step in fulfilling Kittel's vision for a movement he calls Pure Salvage Living. Located in Luling, Texas, the 43 acres of land he has been holding and developing has been coined 'Salvage, Texas', with the aim of becoming a sustainable, self-sufficient village created from 95 per cent salvage.

'This is not profound wisdom, but common sense,' says Kittel. 'Fifty per cent of our landfills in America are composed of building materials. Ancient trees that were hundreds of years old were cut down and turned into buildings, barns and houses that can be salvaged and used once more. We could turn half of that into a generation of houses that will last six times as long as the toxic new building materials that dominate the housing industry today, while creating jobs across the country in the process.'

With over 75 houses built, some of Kittel's houses have been shipped offsite and others are used as guesthouses with an Airbnb operation in place. A trend for tiny houses is taking the world by storm, and Kittel is passionate about teaching others how to build their own from salvage. He is also in the process of setting up Salvagefaire Market, selling all things old, salvaged and crafted in America, as well as an event venue for film and music festivals that would service the 18 million people who live within a ninety-minute drive. Kittel says, 'Those who have lived in the houses have applauded their energy efficiency, but more the quality of life and the love they develop for the house. Unlike those made of sheetrock, concrete, steel and glass, there is an energy that comes with a house made from organic materials. People who stay in them rave about the quality of sleep, the dreams, the feel.'

He adds, 'Creating one-of-a-kind tiny houses out of 95 per cent pure salvage ought to be a globally supported goal. With sustainability as their core ethos, these villages promote a simpler lifestyle than the American Dream that so many were sold and are now sick from. Millions of Americans are coming into retirement, at a rate of around 10,000 per day. These are the invisible Americans who need the jobs and homes that tiny houses could open up to them. We need to create an alternative for the generations that follow.'

RENOVATE **INNOVATE**

page 79: The Mascot is a 10 x 16 foot classic batten-board-style house with a porch view. It was the first Tiny Texas House built by Kittel and is composed of an open living space, bathroom and loft. Apart from electrical parts, plumbing, nails, screws and insulation materials, all the houses are built entirely from salvage.

page 80, top left: Vicky Won is the second Tiny Texas House that was built. It has twin beds on the ground level and a queen bed in the loft, as well as a sink and WC.

page 80, top right: The interior of Vesper Casa contains antique furnishings and a mix of eight species of wood, including longleaf pine, live oak and mesquite. Deer and elk antlers were provided by the client. These were combined with grapevines to create an organic stairwell and railing. A small bathroom window is made from a sewing machine bottom and an old bread pan is used as a spice rack.

page 80, bottom: The Monty Grand Victorian is one of the larger tiny houses, at 900 square feet over two floors. It also boasts a trundle bed that converts to a king size, with closets on either side and a marble bathroom sink with vintage taps.

page 81, top and bottom right: Vicky Too, Vicky Zebu and Arched Zebu. The parts that make up the Zebu sisters were salvaged from 25 different houses. The lumber, siding, floors and roofs are around 200 years old.

page 81, bottom left: At just 63 square feet, Gingered Swan is one of the smallest Tiny Texas Houses available for rental and is completely off grid. Guests are provided with a lantern and have access to a separate bathhouse.

page 82, top: Arched Zebu (as before).

page 82, bottom: The Groom being transported to a new location.

EL MIRADOR **H⊘USE**

CC ARQUITECTOS | STATE OF MEXICO, MEXICO

Manuel Cervantes Céspedes graduated as an architect from Mexico's Anahauc del Norte University. He founded his firm CC Arquitectos in 2004 and, in 2006, began to focus on urban and mass transport projects. Following his work on the Azteca and El Rosario Multimodal Terminals, he has become a leading voice in this sector internationally.

El Mirador house is located on the 95-hectare private property of El Eterno in Valle de Bravo, approximately 156 kilometres southwest of Mexico City. Situated on a mountain slope, the house overlooks stunning views of Lake Avándaro.

'In order to optimize respect for the forest, the building is sunk into the mountainside, gripping to its topography and reducing its impact,' says Cervantes Céspedes. 'I was immediately excited at the opportunity to build in the middle of a wood; I have always been interested in architecture that appears to emerge out of the landscape.'

On the roof of the tucked-away house is the only structure that's visible from the road, a beautiful pavilion clad in repurposed railway sleepers that were sourced from Chihuahua, in the north of Mexico. Cervantes Céspedes's design is based around a series of metal frames that form part of the building's structure while also holding the sleepers in place. The frames also support the mezzanine and wooden roof beams, leaving the entire system exposed on one side. The striking pavilion gives the house its distinctive character, but also functions as a shelter and stable for horses and a garage for concealing parked cars.

The idea to somehow incorporate the railway sleepers into the design originally came from the client. He offered the materials to the architect as he was also using them to build a perimeter wall for the property. In addition to utilizing the sleepers, the architect created a water feature from a roof system that collects rainwater. Inside the shelter, a water trough for the horses sits at one end and a large rectangular pool of water containing a sculpture runs parallel to it. The pool creates stunning reflections of the surrounding forest.

Inside, the domestic spaces of El Mirador house are protected from the climatic conditions, due to it being half buried on one side. A large room that expands out onto the main terrace offers a seamless connection with the outdoors. On one side of the living space is a bedroom with an en suite and, on the other, a second bathroom and kitchen.

Cervantes Céspedes says, 'The various stones used for the paving, as well as the tones and textures of the interior, all blend into the woodland, with an aim to remain unaffected by the passage of time. Earth accumulating between the joints of the materials allows for the sporadic growth of plants and moss, changing the context according to the season. Nature, views and rustic finishes are the main components of the project, whose goal is that these characteristics will endure.'

PHOTOS

page 85: Reclaimed railway sleepers sourced from Chihuahua, north Mexico, were used for the pavilion exterior at El Mirador House. The client also used the sleepers to create a perimeter wall around the property.

page 86: The sunken structure is a 459-square-metre residence built from a combination of steel and wooden beams, with the retaining walls made out of stone sourced from the local area.

page 87, top: The client enjoys entertaining, so a relaxed layout was designed with a social area expanding onto the main terrace. An elegant colour palette of neutral shades was chosen for the interior furnishings.

page 88: The roof of the pavilion collects rainwater and creates a water feature in the process. A sculpture was placed in the large pool, creating a dramatic silhouette by night.

see also pages 10–11: A water trough for horses runs parallel to the water pool.

THE HEMLOFT

JOEL ALLEN | WHISTLER, CANADA

Joel Allen is a former software developer turned carpenter. The idea to build a treehouse initially stemmed from a competition he started with his friend Ryan, which they decided to call 'sport sleeping'. Attempting to outdo Ryan by sleeping in the most outrageous of places, he found the experiences of sleeping in tractor buckets, scaffolding and water towers exhilarating (despite the quality of sleep). He soon came to the conclusion that his preferred locations were high up on a perch, which gave him the idea of creating a more long-term sleeping solution.

Disenchanted by the clunkiness of a conventional treehouse, Allen decided he wanted to create something more elegant. With the help of two architecture graduate friends, the idea of an egg shape was proposed and, after a foam model and 3D rendering confirmed the design would work, Allen made a scaled-down version. He then carried out a stress test on a tree that was just 3 feet tall. 'I was convinced that the full-scale version would easily support a family of black bears, should they decide to inhabit it as a winter hibernation spot,' he says.

Allen spent months searching for the perfect tree on crown land in the backwoods of Whistler, eventually choosing a familiar spot where he felt at home. When he started building, he began framing the HemLoft with new materials, but soon realized he would never be able to afford the $15,000 in materials that it would take to finish it. One evening, he discovered a wealth of free items listed on Craigslist Vancouver, including cedar wood from a dismantled sauna. He ended up trawling through the free section for four months straight, eventually collecting enough materials to finish the project.

'I had a very clear idea of what I wanted my design to be and I looked for materials that would fit the vision,' he explains. 'If you were to look at what I had collected before it was repurposed, it resembled the beginnings of a junkyard, but I had a very specific purpose for each part of each piece. When using salvaged materials, the end result is more satisfying because it's like solving a puzzle that requires patience, persistence and skill. The biggest challenge with this method is that it's difficult to proceed at the pace that you'd like. Sometimes you have to wait for the perfect piece to come along. Fear of missing an opportunity can also lead to collecting for future projects that may never happen. I personally believe this is a trap and one should only collect materials for the projects at hand and let others benefit from the rest.'

He adds, 'Our world can't handle the current rate of waste, so we need those who set the trends to make some level of reuse an industry standard. This needs to be supported by huge salvage warehouses that can save time for industry professionals. The alternative is the longer and more serendipitous route of waiting for the right opportunities to present themselves. It's special when you take a thing that someone else threw away and turn it into something beautiful. I think looking at things for their potential is an optimistic way to see the world.'

RENOVATE **INNOVATE**

RECLAIMED

PHOTOS

page 91: Allen's HemLoft was built on crown land in the backwoods of Whistler, Canada, with a southwestern aspect. He designed it to be like a camping spot, visited from time to time. Reclaimed materials include clear vertical grain cedar for siding, which came from an old sauna, an ash hardwood floor and millwork rebuilt from discarded cabinets, all of which were sourced from Craigslist Vancouver.

page 92, top: Pop-up windows at the top of the structure bring in light and ventilation. All the glass used in the structure was cut from salvaged windows.

page 92, bottom: After making an egg-shaped prototype, Allen built the HemLoft slightly rounder so that it would feel more spacious from the inside.

page 93, top: Apart from paint and fasteners, all other materials were reclaimed. Holes in the stair treads already existed in some of the salvaged boards, so Allen continued the pattern in the other treads to match.

page 93, bottom: View of the Tantalus Mountain Range from the HemLoft.

page 94: As the loft's location became better known, Allen decided to donate it to the owner of Canadian Wilderness Adventures, Alan Crawford. Crawford has plans to resurrect it in an old-growth tree overlooking the Callaghan River, with entry via zipline.

REVIVED

YORK HOUSE APARTMENT

PATRICK LEWIS ARCHITECTS LTD | LONDON, UNITED KINGDOM

York House is a Victorian mansion block located in central London's Marylebone neighbourhood. A four-bedroom apartment on its second floor had been lived in by the same family for 40 years but had not been refurbished for nearly half a century. The new owners were from Los Angeles and in need of a London base. Patrick Lewis Architects were given the task of remodelling it for contemporary living, while making the most of its light and proportions.

Structural works involved knocking down a wall between the dining room and living room before moving the old kitchen to the front of the property, where it could benefit from more light. One bedroom was converted into two en suite bathrooms and the old kitchen subsequently became a bedroom. The new layout creates a striking vista all the way through the building, which can be appreciated immediately upon entering.

Because the property was intended to be used as a pied-à-terre, areas like the kitchen didn't require large amounts of storage, which allowed for more freedom in the design. An eclectic mix of vintage objects and furniture pieces were set off against each other by being carefully placed against a modest backdrop.

The client had a strong aesthetic and shared Patrick Lewis's enthusiasm for reclaimed materials. Sourced mainly from London and Oxford, these resources also meant the team could be more creative with the budget. Along with the salvaged elements, economic tiles on the walls were balanced with more expensive bathroom fittings. The reclaimed kitchen sink originally would have been used for washing laundry and the wardrobe doors in the bedroom were made from cheese boards. Other experimental pieces included bespoke window shutters carefully crafted from a spliced Georgian door, while the use of reclaimed double doors as an alternative to making them new meant a substantial amount of money was saved. Lewis remarks, 'Working with old materials and objects is interesting because there is a skill to controlling the juxtaposition of different species of timber, for example, and seeing how they work against each other.'

The apartment is furnished with pieces that the owners collected over the years, and some of the strip flooring was reclaimed from the BBC's old premises in White City. This has a special meaning for the clients, who work in film and television. Lewis explains, 'I am particularly interested in the sustainable aspect of reusing something that has already had a life, but also because of the embodied memory of an object. Being able to create a more emotional connection to the person who lives in a space is, I think, a lot to do with the reclaimed palette. It is more difficult to make something from reclaimed materials because nothing is straight, it has moisture content, everything moves about and it's more taxing, but you need to embrace that. To take apart an original door carefully enough to keep it intact takes an enormous amount of skill. A lot of people are unaware of that or are scared of it, but there are huge gains to this way of working. It's a situation where the joiner says, are you sure you really want to do this? But afterwards, everyone falls in love with the end result.'

RENOVATE **INNOVATE**

PHOTOS

page 99: The client's vintage and antique pieces are set against walls painted in Farrow & Ball's Hardwick White.

page 100, top left: Industrial pieces were incorporated into the kitchen, including vintage factory lighting and exposed copper taps. The reclaimed laundry maid's sink would once have been used for washing clothes.

page 100, top right: The bright blue glazed partition doors selected for York House Apartment demonstrate its owner's brave sense of colour. These contrast with encaustic hand-made Tuscan terracotta tiles found at a reclamation yard in Oxford.

page 100, bottom left: Reclaimed Georgian doors sourced from LASSCO were spliced down the middle and made into shutters.

page 100, bottom right: The vintage fretwork light fittings are repurposed and would have originally been an architectural detail.

page 101: Reclaimed double doors direct the view through the property. Modern white flooring bounces natural light back into the room.

page 102: Reclaimed wood used for the wardrobe doors was once cheese boards. The strip flooring in the bathroom was salvaged from the BBC's old headquarters in White City.

THE WHITE HOUSE

WT ARCHITECTURE | ISLE OF COLL, SCOTLAND, UNITED KINGDOM

Constructed in the mid-1700s, this square-cornered limestone dwelling was the first of its kind on the Isle of Coll in Scotland. The house was built by the Macleans of Coll, a branch of the Maclean clan who inhabited the island for hundreds of years. Home to their estate manager, it was informally known as The White House since houses on the island were typically black during that time. In 1773, the imposing structure was visited by the English writer Samuel Johnson while on his tour of the Hebrides with James Boswell. Because the house was built on sand, however, it was not long before it began to crack, and it was abandoned by the mid-1800s.

One hundred and fifty years later it was inherited by Alex and Seonaid Maclean-Bristol, by which time the ruin had no roof and its cracks were more than a foot wide; the basic structure, however, had remained intact. The couple were keen to create a family home on the site but were not sure whether to restore the ruin or build a separate house nearby. It was suggested by William Tunnell of WT Architecture that they instead explore the possibility of partially occupying the ruin with new accommodation connected to it. As Tunnell describes it, 'Essentially, it was an ordinary Georgian three-bay, two-storey building. What made it interesting was that the walls were exceptionally thick and it was starting to fall down. From a design point of view, the biggest challenge was not only to stabilize the building, but to guard against over-sanitizing it with a new structure. It needed to have a sense of belonging both in terms of the building and the landscape and we didn't want to eclipse the intangible qualities of the original ruin. It was important that it still had a sense that the front door was the old front door and that you were drawn to that, rather than being drawn to something new behind it.'

The project began with a six-month consolidation period, whereby the existing ruin was stabilized by a local island builder. Due to the remoteness of the site and exposure to the elements, meticulous planning was crucial. Imported aggregate and masonry were kept to a minimum to reduce transportation and environmental costs. With only three ferries a week operating to the island in winter, combined with sometimes brutal weather conditions, the clients often provided food and accommodation to contractors in the nearby farmhouse they were staying in.

Although it was possible to stabilize the building's sizeable fractures, there was no easy way to close them up. It was ultimately decided that, because they contributed so much to the identity of the house, they should be left intact. The original stone enclosure walls around the house were extended with recycled rubble from the site and black stained timber was used to make the new construction recede and ensure that, from a distance, the stone elements remained visually prevalent.

'With an edifice as rich and historically significant as The White House, there is plenty to respond to,' Tunnell says. 'When working with an existing building, there may be lots of unwelcome strictures and challenges, but where there is an existing context, both emotionally and viscerally – how a window is framing an amazing view or a wall is providing shelter – you are provided with a whole raft of opportunities.'

PHOTOS

page 105: Preserving the cracked gable meant the White House ruin retained its dramatic and imposing character. This is stitched up with stainless steel ties about 2–3 metres long that are embedded into the walls on either side, going up like a corset.

page 106, top: Since the Isle of Coll is so far north, the winter days can be very short. The orientation of the glass windows was key to maximizing the low-slung sunlight for as long as possible.

page 106, bottom: The main ruin houses the entrance hall, kitchen and master bedroom as well as a larder, WC, shower room, study and storage area. The plan was designed in an H-shape, which externally creates pockets of shelter on a very exposed site. Stone walls extended from the ruin were built up, providing enclosures that the new structure could nestle in, and half of the original house was also kept roofless, forming a courtyard garden.

page 107, top: Living spaces and bedrooms are surrounded by ample glazing, boasting stunning landscape and sea views of Rough Bay, also known as Grishipol. The building is heated through a heat exchanger, with energy produced by three wind turbines located on the hill opposite.

page 107, bottom: The house offers both expansive and intimate spaces. A wing of new rooms to the west provides four further bedrooms, utility spaces and a panelled snug space, which is separated from the main living room by a wall of shelves.

page 108: The book-lined landing has a long window seat that looks out over the big sheltering west wall and down to the owner's boat mooring.

TINY HOUSE

JESSICA HELGERSON INTERIOR DESIGN | OREGON, UNITED STATES

Jessica Helgerson is a Portland-based designer of residential and commercial interiors. With a long-standing interest in green building and sustainability, she has sat on a number of boards devoted to environmental preservation. In 2008, Helgerson and her husband bought a 540-square-foot cottage on five acres of farmland on Sauvie Island, an agricultural landmass on the Columbia River just north of Portland. The cottage was first built in the early 1940s as part of Vanport Village, a development constructed to house shipyard workers from Vancouver in Washington and Portland. When Vanport Village flooded in 1948, the small structure floated down the river to Sauvie Island, where it became the goose check station (a place where hunters would showcase the geese they had shot). Years later, it was remodelled and became a rental property.

Helgerson's redesign was the fourth time the house had been renovated. As with most of her projects, her goal was to ensure the fundamental design and materials were classic and long-lasting, as well as being appropriate for the building and its period. Rather then extending the property, they chose to work with its existing size. Retaining only the exterior walls, the windows, doors, roof and interior were replaced almost entirely with reclaimed materials, a decision based on a combination of what looked right for the property and what was immediately on hand. 'Mostly we were trying to do something beautiful and economical that felt right for the place,' says Helgerson. 'We love to work on old buildings because it really makes us respond in fresh ways to the existing conditions. I think when designing only new buildings, it's easy to get formulaic. I hate to see great old buildings get torn down and replaced with ugly new ones. It seems so sad, and a waste.'

Given its small footprint, Helgerson redesigned the interior of Tiny House for maximum efficiency, creating one open-plan room that comprises the dining room, living room and kitchen. This room also contains built-in sofas that double as twin beds for guests, and hidden storage underneath provides an ideal place for children's toys. The ceiling of the main living area was opened up to give a feeling of space, but lowered over the bathroom and bedroom to make a lofted sleeping area for adults accessed via a walnut ladder. A wall of shelving provides plenty of room for books and large, low-set windows bring ample light into the interior.

The family spent four years living in the cottage. Raising chickens, turkeys and bees, they have worked towards self-sufficiency, with nearly everything they eat grown at home. A 1,200-square-foot greenhouse on the site houses vegetable gardens and fruit trees, and they're even able to make cheese from a neighbour's goats and cows. They now live in a larger house on the same property, making the cottage the perfect place for relatives and friends to stay.

PHOTOS

page 111: One addition to the 1940s Tiny House was a green roof, which was planted with moss and ferns gathered from the Columbia River gorge.

page 112, top: Tall, high-efficiency windows come right down to sofa level, letting in maximum light.

page 112, bottom: One wall contains the kitchen, maximizing the available space. The range is a vintage Craigslist find, the dining table is made from locally salvaged walnut and the chairs are vintage Paul McCobb.

page 113, top, and bottom right: The parents' bedroom is located on the mezzanine level of the main room, which is lined with vintage Moroccan Beni Ourain rugs and accessed via a walnut ladder. In addition to a separate kids' bedroom, the built-in sofas double up as beds for guests. The floors are local Oregon white oak.

page 113, bottom left: The bathtub was rescued from a friend's demolition site.

page 114: The walls were insulated, then faced in reclaimed wood siding from a barn that had been deconstructed onsite.

MILANESE APARTMENT

THE CHIC FISH | MILAN, ITALY

Husband and wife duo Giovanni Gennari and Anna Carbone are co-founders of design studio The Chic Fish, which they started up in 2015. Recognized as trend-setters for an aesthetic they describe as 'contemporary vintage', the studio focuses on finding creative solutions for branding, interior design and set design. The Chic Fish originally began as a blog in 2011, and continues to research and document the couple's love of beautiful vintage design. Gennari's background is in marketing and communication; he has worked for companies such as McCann and Discovery Networks. Carbone was previously Design Director for the Italian branding agency Robilant & Associati.

With their vision defined by a penchant for coolhunting and a fresh take on vintage, it's no surprise that the interior of the couple's early 19th-century home demonstrates an expert blend of traditional styles with a modern kind of beauty. Carbone says, 'The renovation project was based on a very tight concept that reflected our way of being and living: to create a home that tells the story of the people who live there.'

Much of the exposed original fabric of the building was deliberately left as the couple found it. Carbone explains, 'Instead of adding layers and matter, we subtracted. We wanted to highlight the ancient floors, leave the old fixtures untouched and bring to light the apartment's history through the peeling walls and stratification of previous restructure. An intervention of the industrial into a middle-class house creates an interesting contrast and an ideal backdrop for vintage furniture and other unique pieces we create with our valued craftsmen.'

Almost everything in the house is vintage, including signed works of modern art found in flea markets, always chosen with love. The reclaimed floor tiles were salvaged from other old apartments and parquet flooring was crafted from salvaged scaffolding boards. The large steel structure that separates the living room from the kitchen is a restored vintage window frame recovered from the old Fiat factory in Lingotto, Turin. 'It allows you to have two separate rooms but with the advantages of light and open space,' says Gennari.

The home's aesthetic is achieved through a clever mix of older and newer elements. Colours and materials deliberately alternate, breaking up a scheme that would otherwise be too linear or logical. Recovered forms and objects are also positioned in a way that is never predictable and creates contrast. 'We try to work more with emotions than with stuff,' Gennari explains. 'We are affected by what an object evokes, its history, design and what it reminds us of. Of course, we always have so much fun in making, restoring or giving new uses to things. Upcycling is a very interesting topic at present and will have a significant effect on the world our children grow up in. Everything produced has the potential for a second life and it doesn't make sense to throw away something that can be used by someone else. As well as respecting the environment, it also develops ingenuity. It is definitely one of the great themes of design.'

PHOTOS

page 117: The Milanese Apartment is located on the second floor of a building constructed in the early 1800s. The kitchen and living room are separated by a screen made from a restored steel frame, sourced from the old Fiat factory in Turin. Old electric cables were left intact.

page 118: The flooring is a mix of hexagonal reclaimed tiles and salvaged scaffolding boards that create a parquet pattern. Key pieces include an original leather Chesterfield sofa, a pharmacy sign sourced from Naples and Bufferlamp porcelain pendant lights by Wieki Somers for Pols Potten.

page 119: The table is made from a slab of cedar with an iron base beneath, a bespoke piece created by the couple. The anatomy poster was sourced from an antique shop in Berlin.

page 120: The house is full of items that tell the story of its owners, many of which were picked up on their travels. Four antique oratory seats line the main entrance, along with a set of antique mirrors. The vintage pendant lights were bought at a flea market in Brooklyn.

see also page 2: A vintage poster of Moira Orfei hangs on stripped back walls.

ASTLEY CASTLE

WITHERFORD WATSON MANN | WARWICKSHIRE, UNITED KINGDOM

Astley Castle, near Nuneaton in Warwickshire, is a Grade II* listed building which has been occupied since at least AD 1200. Additions were made to its medieval core in the 15th and 17th centuries and, in more recent times, the castle was used as a hotel until a fire in 1978 left it derelict. In the early 2000s, the Landmark Trust launched a competition to turn the ruin into a house that would be suitable for holiday accommodation while making the most of its historic remains. The winners were architects Witherford Watson Mann, who went on to win the 2013 RIBA Stirling Prize for the project.

The Landmark Trust advised that the new building should complement the existing structure and enhance enjoyment of its natural and notable features in all seasons. For architect William Mann, the challenge was working out how to achieve a balance between retaining the ruinous character and creating the warm qualities of a home. One approach would have been to restore the ruin as a detached structure and place a new building inside it, but for Mann, this was not the optimal solution. Instead of inserting geometric new elements, new walls were built directly on to the existing ones, with the new bricks in direct contact with the craggy edges of the original stone. Only a third of the castle contains living quarters, which are surrounded by roofless courtyards. This approach maximizes the vistas through the building, as well as the drama of the ruin. With the addition of long windows and furnishings in rich, warm colours inside, the required feeling of domestic comfort is achieved.

Mann, who has experience working on a number of adaptive reuse projects, believes the new is seldom a clean break with the past, but is more often an evolution of it. 'When you work on existing buildings you sacrifice many apparent freedoms of new-build but, in our view, you can gain more than you lose,' he says. 'Existing buildings carry environmental, social and cultural capital. They are in their users' memories and imaginations; they articulate and are identified with a set of values. There's something very appealing about achieving maximum social and economic impact with a minimum of intervention and addition, a kind of conceptual elegance that happens also to be environmentally and socially responsible.'

PHOTOS

page 123: The rooms of Astley Castle are surrounded by a series of partially roofed external courts. The ruin acts like a sundial, as the patterns of shadow and light shift throughout the day.

page 124, top: The window designs were influenced by the Gothic proportions of the castle openings. They are set deep in the reveal so that the play of shadows isn't disturbed by a reflective plane.

page 124, bottom left: Some of the existing fabric of the ruin is around 600 years old. A harmonious colour palette was created with charcoal-fired bricks which echo the reds and greens of the sandstone and limestone.

page 124, bottom right: On the first floor the low kitchen niche is asymmetric, narrowing on the right as it goes up, in the manner of a medieval fireplace.

page 125: Crumbling ancient masonry walls were stabilized with resin anchors, ttied together with new concrete lintels and edged, capped and buttressed by new brickwork.

pages 126–7: The accommodation inhabits the oldest part of the castle, the early medieval fortified manor. It has an inverted layout with bedrooms on the ground floor and living spaces on the first floor.

page 128: The stairs are realized in oak with open treads. The timber elements are ordered and assembled, in contrast with the soft, crafted masonry.

see also pages 96–7: Stained softwood, limed oak, bronze anodized aluminium and bronze-painted steel were used in the room interiors of Astley Castle. Furnishings by John Evetts include deep copper and green curtains with rust-coloured fabrics.

EIXAMPLE APARTMENT

EO ARQUITECTURA | BARCELONA, SPAIN

EO Arquitectura are a young multidisciplinary office based in Barcelona, founded by Clara Ocana and Adrian Elizalde. In 2014 they were tasked with transforming a 70-square-foot residence in a 1930s building situated in the city's Eixample neighbourhood, a stone's throw from Gaudí's famous Sagrada Família. The two-bedroom property was intended to be rented out for both long- and short-term periods so there was freedom to design the space however they saw fit, providing the result was attractive and achieved on a very limited budget.

The apartment already featured traditional vaulted ceilings and beautiful patterned mosaic tile floors made using old Catalonian hydraulic tiles (named as such because a hydraulic machine is used to introduce colour to them). Given their aim to maximize profit by using what was previously there, the decision to preserve the existing floors was economical as well as aesthetic. Ripping out the tiles and replacing them would have been costly, so they studied each of them individually and painstakingly repaired as many as they could.

'The apartment presented a decayed and dark image due to excessive subdivided rooms,' Elizalde says. 'Different layers of materials and installations had built up over the years, so the main action we took was a selective defoliation or "undressing" of all the layers, in order to reach the traditional elements of the building. Our intervention seeks to redraw the traditional architecture of the Eixample. We tried to make a contemporary space without losing the essence of the traditional. The result is harmonious and timeless, where old and new mix together.'

Many of the apartment's design features were influenced by a trip that Elizalde and Ocana took to Japan in 2014. The main living area is a multifunctional space with a large table forming its heart, inspired by a project called Tables for a Restaurant by Japanese architect Junya Ishigami. At over 3 metres long, the table is in close proximity to the living room, master bedroom and kitchen and can act as both a study area and dining table.

Another feature typically found in both ancient and contemporary Japanese culture is the sliding door system. This creates flexible interior boundaries and diffuses the sense of confinement. 'We can transform the space to provide necessary privacy, greater intimacy or open everything up and expand the space,' says Elizalde. 'Renovating an existing space allows you to feel the beauty of the passage of time. Old buildings were more handcrafted and it is very special to think that, many years ago, different people and different societies used that space. It offers the possibility to combine different topics, add complexity and give a special meaning to the final product.'

RENOVATE **INNOVATE**

PHOTOS

page 131: The table inside the Eixample Apartment is 3.1 metres long and is inspired by the work of Junya Ishigami. Modern, industrial-style lighting hangs from the vaulted ceiling.

page 132, top: A bench 5.2 metres long runs along the side wall, providing seating for the table as well as shelving and storage space. The redesign allows for additional storage space to be added if necessary, providing flexibility for the owners.

page 132, bottom left: The existing traditional Catalonian patterned tiles mark out the original layout of the apartment, revealing how the rooms were once divided.

page 132, bottom right: The apartment balcony overlooks the street, also offering views of Barcelona's famous landmark, La Sagrada Família by Antoni Gaudí.

page 133: The sliding wooden doors provide flexibility and enhance the feeling of light and space when opened up.

page 134: The apartment is painted white throughout to maximize the natural light and draw attention to the colours in the floor tiles. An interior window lets natural light into the bedroom when the doors are closed.

RUSSELL–FONTANEZ
APARTMENT

LOT-EK | NEW YORK, UNITED STATES

LOT-EK is an award-winning architectural design studio founded by Ada Tolla and Giuseppe Lignano, based in New York and Naples, Italy. Renowned for its research into innovative ways of conserving materials and energy, the studio also specializes in the upcycling of industrial objects and systems, such as shipping containers. 'Arriving in the US, we were immediately inspired by the presence and abundance of the manmade,' says Tolla. 'We started thinking about the meaning of working as architects now, in cities, for cities. How could we mine such a manmade landscape? How could we take from everything that we already produce and use those same objects as the raw materials of architecture? We collected leftovers and brought them into our studio to investigate their potential. Somehow, we managed to look at those objects outside of their meaning, cultural significance and scale. We looked at their volume, structure, form, we tilted them upside-down and inside-out, we tested ideas, we transformed them and were immediately intrigued by the results.'

In 2010 LOT-EK were asked to design and revamp an East Village apartment housed in a small pre-war tenement building that became co-op in the early 1980s. The apartments on each floor had been cheaply renovated, with two small single units turned into one, encircling a central staircase. This had resulted in a difficult layout, with dark spaces, awkward connections and wasted space. The clients wanted to create a modern, open-plan dwelling with more light, functional areas and storage. Tolla and Lignano's solution was to transform the least interesting areas into main features.

After they demolished unnecessary party walls, two tunnels were created on either side of the staircase to make use of the dead space. The tunnels were lined with 63 upcycled commercial steel doors which were painted a vibrant shade of red. Utilities were moved to the centre of the apartment, freeing up the front and rear spaces. Two bathrooms, a wardrobe, a laundry and a storage area are accessed by the narrower of the two tunnels. The wider tunnel houses a dining area, with a custom-made table that LOT-EK designed from reclaimed sassafras and steel. An upholstered banquette provides seating on one side of the table (and also includes hidden storage).

Interior design such as this demonstrates LOT-EK's interest in seeing cities, buildings and spaces as layers. Tolla explains, 'Objects carry their life and DNA. They carry their layers – we just add one more. In the work of upcycling, I would argue that they are not really "materials" any longer. We transform objects through operations, which are both physical and conceptual. The intervention leads to unknown and surprising experiences of space, use and colour. We like to look at something that makes you ask questions about provenance, economy, politics, production and humanity. There is finally a serious interest in upcycling and a sense of urgency, which is great and long overdue. In architecture, though, we have to fight the fight. The construction industry is inherently tied to the "standard" and the conventional, and there is a lot to do in order to pry that open. But we are very excited and proud to be working on that battleground.'

RENOVATE **INNOVATE**

PHOTOS

page 137: The larger of the two tunnels inside the Russell-Fontanez Apartment contains a custom-made dining table which comfortably seats 12. The upholstered banquette, also crafted from reclaimed steel doors, has extra storage inside. Original details of the doors, including hinges and signs of wear on the ends, were deliberately kept to create an industrial feel and contrast with the more finished details.

page 138, top: The shade of paint used on the doors is called Safety Red by Benjamin Moore.

page 138, bottom: The new configuration means the rooms at either end of the tunnels are more calm and spacious.

page 139, top: The galley kitchen that was once in the hallway was moved to where the former dining room used to stand. It features stainless steel cabinets and Corian worktops.

page 139, bottom: The enamelled glossy red bounces natural light back into the space, giving the apartment a warm aura.

page 140: Cutouts were created in the doors where the handles and locks used to be, providing an ideal place for light fittings. Storage space, cupboards, bathrooms and a laundry area are all accessed via the tunnels.

Quintana Partners design studio is comprised of Benito Escat Diaz, his son Benito Escat Velez and Pol Castells Segarra. Originally from Barcelona, the elder Diaz worked in watchmaking for many years before launching a career in interior design. Involved with various restoration projects in destinations such as Frankfurt, Miami and Venezuela, he always had a particular fondness for the architecture of Menorca. After visiting every summer, he eventually decided to set up his home on the island, where the Quintana Partners studio is based. The team now works predominantly on renovation and interior design projects in both Barcelona and Menorca.

Home B is contained in a building that dates back to the 18th century, when Menorca was still a British colony. In the 1930s, a local architect remodelled it into a casino and café. Occupying the whole of the ground floor, it was considered one of the most modern cafés in town due to being tiled throughout. It became a meeting point for the Republicans during the Spanish Civil War and was later ordered to be shut down by the dictator Francisco Franco. In its place a business selling lamps opened up, until Diaz took on the building and turned it into his home.

In keeping with the Quintana Partners' aesthetic, the original fabric of the house has remained largely untouched. Even the additional kitchen and bathroom renovations that were made in the 1960s were kept intact, with a view to preserving the history of the building in its entirety. Diaz says, 'We stripped back the walls to find authentic materials. In some cases we found original paintings and frescoes. The renovation respects all the materials and architectural features that have existed in the house for more than 200 years. Rather than creating more waste, we always want to restore the original, which means we don't have to buy more and contaminate the planet. We try to be as ecological as possible.'

The house has a a layout typical of the English colonial style, reflected in the many small bedrooms and the stairwell, from which all the rooms can be accessed. New pipes and electricity, as well as a new bathroom on the top floor, provide 21st-century comforts. The most interesting intervention, however, is the vast collection of art, objects and priceless furniture that decorate the house, making it an enormous cabinet of curiosities. The visual concoction of vintage and antique pieces ranges from video arcade machines and model aeroplanes to religious iconography, skulls and animal skin rugs. All the items have been collected by Diaz over the years and provide daily delight, inspiration and amusement. 'We are passionate about restoring homes that have seen a lot of life,' he reveals. 'The columns and style of the windows all have a magnificent charm. Combined with the beautiful vintage furniture, Home B captures the memories of a life, but is also a great example of cultural heritage and Menorcan architecture.'

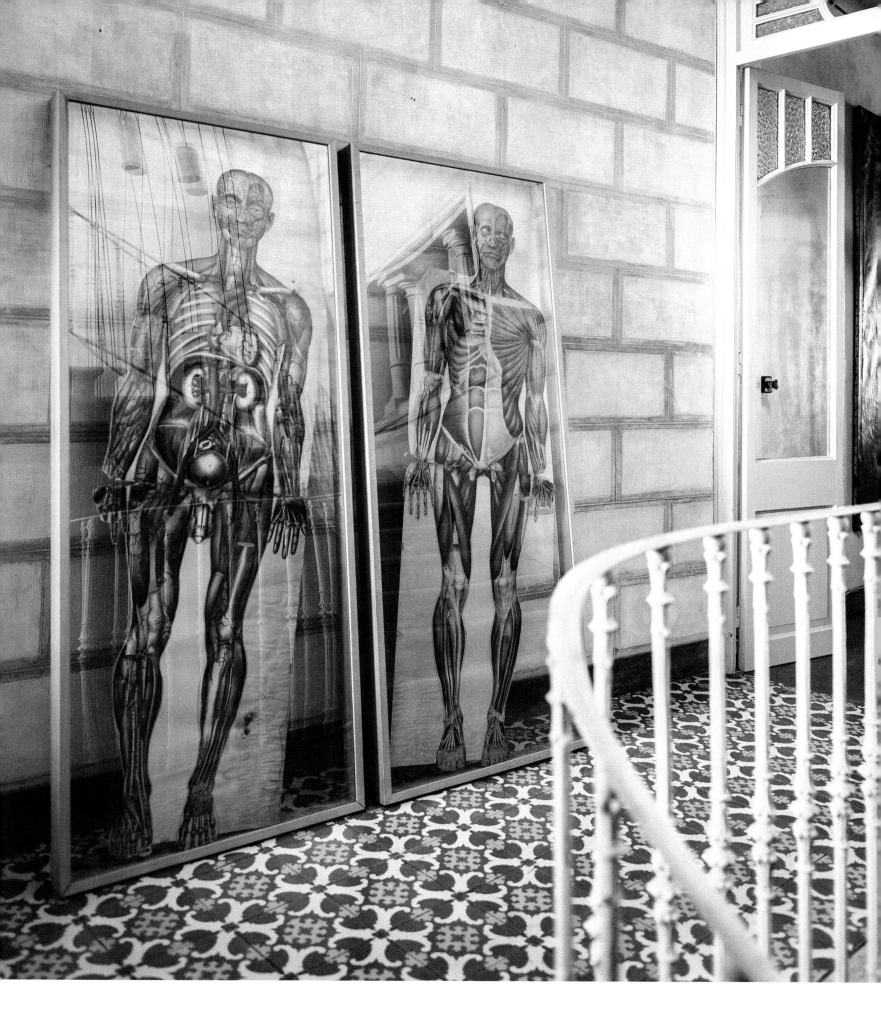

PHOTOS

page 143: The ground floor of Home B still has its original blue-and-white wall tiles from its time as a café in the 1930s.

page 144: Extraordinary vintage pieces are distributed around the house, such as the framed anatomical drawings on the landing.

page 145, top left: The team decided to keep some of the historical refurbishments from over the years, including the 1960s kitchen.

page 145, top right: The attractive stairwell is furnished with a cascading pendant light, a bespoke piece made for the house by Spanish company Santa & Cole.

page 145, bottom: The bathroom's peeling walls and exposed rafters contrast with elegant fittings and a freestanding roll-top bath. Materials such as sandstone and limestone found in the original fabric of the building would have come from Menorcan quarries.

page 146: The three-storey house is a gallery of furniture and objects displayed in unpredictable juxtapositions. Diaz sources his collection from all over the world, mostly from antique shops.

page 147, bottom: The skull with a bird perched on top was bought at an antique shop in Paris. Delicate mouldings and stained glass in the windows and doors reveal the building's English colonial past.

See also pages 254–5.

BERLIN SUMMER APARTMENT

LOFT KOLASIŃSKI | BERLIN, GERMANY

Loft Kolasiński are a team of interior and industrial designers based in Szczecin, the capital city of Poland's West Pomerania Province, on the German–Polish border. Headed up by Jacek Kolasiński, the studio works on interior design projects that often incorporate vintage decorative elements as well as furniture pieces they design in collaboration with artisans.

The Berlin Summer Apartment is located in an old palace, surrounded by forests, in the city's suburbs. The palace was built between 1856 and 1859 and became a hospital in the latter half of the 20th century, during the German Democratic Republic. After the fall of the GDR it became a ruin before eventually being purchased and refurbished.

In this particular part of the palace – a 160-square-metre space on ground level – huge amounts of construction waste had to be removed from all the rooms before it underwent a major renovation. It still had its original threshing floor, so bricks and wooden planks were used to create new flooring throughout. For the interior design, Kolasiński took inspiration from Mediterranean architecture. 'In order to avoid banality, the furnishings were chosen to be a little eccentric, mysterious and elegant, while the kitchen has a simple, homely and rural character,' he explains.

Most of the furniture, lighting and rugs come from Poland and have been combined with other mid-century pieces from Denmark and the Czech Republic. With an address book full of collectors and dealers, the Loft Kolasiński team have been able to acquire many unusual vintage pieces over the years. The four grey mid-century upholstered armchairs were bought at auction and required complete restoration. They are very rare pieces that were manufactured in a small factory in Zadziele, near Żywiec, in south-central Poland. The factory originally specialized in the Bauhaus style but the authorities deemed its products too avant-garde, so it was subsequently forced to produce only medical furniture.

The cavernous rooms were painted crisp white, which highlights the characterful vaulted ceilings, some of which were left unpainted. Doors were removed in order to open the space up, allowing the original architecture to provide attractive vistas through the apartment. Various nooks in the communal spaces also create a perfect stage for the carefully selected vintage furniture pieces. In the kitchen, exposed light fittings, stainless steel freestanding units and a bespoke table made from vintage standing hairdryers bring an industrial twist to the scheme.

Kolasiński says, 'We have worked on many unusual properties, including the adaptation of industrial buildings, attics and old houses. In general, we use our experience and sense of space to create the perfect balance between old and new. It is also important that most of the new items in our projects, usually furniture, are designed by our studio. Design has come full circle, so it is now difficult to design something that is completely new. I think this means restoration will become more and more popular. Currently, it is hard to find skilled craftsmen, which means vintage furniture that was crafted using traditional methods of joinery will be considered increasingly more valuable.'

RENOVATE **INNOVATE**

PHOTOS

page 151: Geometric furnishings and fittings contrast with the curved arches and rough texture of the white painted walls in the Berlin Summer Apartment.

page 152, top: The poster in the dining room is by Polish graphic designer Wieslaw Walkuski. The sideboard is a bespoke piece from the 1960s, made in the Polish city of Katowice.

page 152, bottom: The large wool carpet in the living room is by Kowary, 1968.

page 153, top: The walls of the apartment were cleaned and covered in a thin layer of plaster before being painted.

page 153, bottom: A red patterned runner leads the eye through the apartment while also bringing warmth to the space.

pages 154–5: The dining table in the kitchen is a bespoke piece designed by Loft Kolasiński and has legs constructed from vintage standing hairdryers. The chandelier in the kitchen is a Polish design from the 1960s–70s. The flooring is made from reclaimed wood, salvaged from a house in Poland.

REIMAGINED

ALPINE BARN APARTMENT

OFIS ARCHITECTS | BOHINJ, SLOVENIA

OFIS Architects was founded by Rok Oman and Spela Videčnik in 1996. The practice has an international reach with an award-winning portfolio, ranging from student housing in Paris to Borisov Arena in Belarus. In recent years they have built more than 2,500 housing units. Oman and Videčnik are also visiting lecturers at Harvard University.

Alpine Barn Apartment is a project that embraces tradition, celebrates heritage and sets an example for preserving Slovene vernacular architecture. Many of the barns, hayracks and farmhouses scattered around the area's countryside no longer serve their purpose and, because they are not maintained, are often left to fall into disrepair and replaced with generic housing. OFIS Architects converted this 200-year-old disused cattle barn, located within the Julian Alps in the Upper Carniola region of northwestern Slovenia, into a contemporary retreat. The two-storey holiday cabin retains its original exterior appearance. However, the interior is a fresh and modern space, with walls, floors and furniture all crafted from deep-brushed local spruce.

The 120-square-metre barn originally contained a stable for livestock on the ground level and had a ramp leading up to the first floor, which was used for drying and storing hay, fodder and farm equipment. The existing ramp, which leads to the wooden deck above the cattle area, now serves as the main entrance to the barn.

An open-plan living space on the ground floor is marked out by the existing wooden beam structure, dividing the dining room, living room and bedroom (which sits on a raised platform). Additional spaces such as the wardrobe, bathrooms, sauna, fireplace and kitchen are positioned to one side and disguised behind a vertical wooden plank wall. Inspired by loft spaces, the area inside feels airy and streamlined, made warm and welcoming by the enveloping wooden shell.

Upstairs leads to a gallery overlooking the main living space where a guest bedroom is located. A link to the building's heritage was created with framed photos of wooden details of the barn exterior, which sit among four existing cutout openings in the wall. The former external storage area next to the entrance is converted into a porch overlooking breathtaking views of the Alps.

All the original exterior wooden cladding and concrete roof slates were deliberately maintained. Looking at the barn from the outside, only a hint of modern intervention is signified by the circular perforations in the wooden gable. These can also be found behind the internal windows, a subtle detail that brings dappled patterns of sunlight into the building. As Oman explains, 'The project met our criteria for aesthetics, durability, sustainability, preservation and heritage. These buildings are not protected, so ultimately we wanted to make Alpine Barn Apartment an example to others, deterring them from tearing them down.'

RENOVATE **INNOVATE**

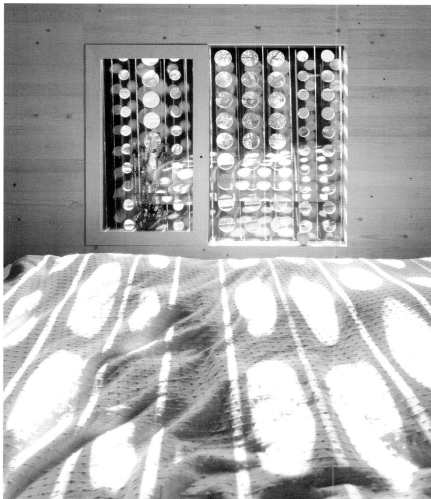

PHOTOS

pages 161 and 163, top left:
A rectangle of circular perforations on the front of the Alpine Barn is the only visible alteration to its exterior. The level underneath the barn houses the service rooms, containing equipment, storage and a garage for one car.

page 162, top: The barn is situated in the Julian Alps and is used as a family guesthouse. It's an archetypal landmark of the Slovenian countryside.

page 162, bottom: The bed, dining suite and seating area are all crafted from deep-brushed local spruce, creating a uniform aesthetic and a sense of being inside a wooden shell.

page 163, top right: The living area extends out onto what was once the external storage area, now converted into a porch.

page 163, bottom left: Stairs lead up to a mezzanine containing a second bedroom area.

page 163, bottom right: Holes in the exterior of the barn bring a play of shadows into the interior.

pages 164–5: The loft-inspired conversion takes advantage of the barn's vast proportions, highlighting the exposed original beams.

page 166: The existing ramp forms the main entrance to the barn.

LIGHT STUDIO

MANOLO YLLERA | MADRID, SPAIN

As soon as you enter the live/work space owned by Spanish interiors photographer Manolo Yllera, his passion for interior design is self-evident. Filled with an imaginative composition of vintage objects, furniture and art which come together beautifully, the loft apartment has brought him almost as much attention as his photographs and has been used as a location for a variety of film and TV productions as well as photoshoots.

With a clear dual purpose in mind, the decision to purchase a loft contained in a building that was once an industrial bakery was purely pragmatic. As a photographer, Yllera required a large and well-lit space that would allow him to move his flash and spotlights easily, but he also needed a place to live. He says, 'Here, I failed all my goals of space saving and practicality. It was hard to find a space in the centre of Madrid without columns in the middle of the rooms and with both a 4.5-metre-high ceiling and lateral light, as well as a clear distinction between spaces: the house and the photography set. The initial idea was to preserve the photography set and make it as clean and empty as possible. The problem was that my passion for decorating was gradually gaining ground.'

Yllera's collection started with an armchair reupholstered with recycled coffee sacks followed by a Louis XV sofa. Before he knew it, there were chairs and carpets filling almost the entire space. 'Every time we needed to do a shoot for a client, we had to move the furniture into the street, or just anywhere. It was a crazy and impractical way of working,' he recalls. Much to Yllera's surprise, it was the decor that brought him a new wave of business and clientele – the space has been used to shoot a number of video clips, films and commercials, with more than 50 sessions used for advertising. He adds, 'I've had people making cooking shows in my kitchen, and models dancing on the sofas. The armchair upholstered with hessian fabric has even been on an album cover.'

Against a sea of white and a floor covered in Moroccan Beni Ourain rugs, the interior decor is an eclectic mix of furniture found on the street, heirlooms and design icons, all in a myriad of styles. Classic chairs sit alongside statement design pieces such as the sculptural Marteen Baas Clay chair in red, with equipment used for Yllera's work interspersed among them. He also chose to have the furniture inherited from his grandmother repainted in a radical way to capture the new spirit of the space, as well as commissioning artist friends to make paintings for the walls, some of which have been done directly on screens and doors.

With growing demand, Yllera was forced to find a small warehouse next to his studio to stock furniture for his productions, enabling him to change the decor for different events. 'In the end, the space took his own voice and made me obey him,' he says. 'This place is a mirror of my life and my profession. Both have converged together in the same spot, a nonsense story with a happy ending.'

RENOVATE **INNOVATE**

REIMAGINED

PHOTOS

page 169: The rusty Tolix chairs inside Yllera's Light Studio were rescued from a skip. Stairs lead up to a mezzanine level where his office is located.

page 170: The coffee table is made from a door that Yllera found in the street.

page 171, top left: The chandelier above the dining table belonged to Yllera's grandmother, as did the old mirror, which has been painted on with a marker.

page 171, top right: The living room area features an armchair upholstered in hessian coffee sacks and a chair made from an upcycled oil barrel.

page 171, bottom: Floors are furnished with Moroccan Beni Ourain rugs throughout.

pages 172–3: Yllera's eclectic mix of found pieces comes together harmoniously against a neutral-coloured background. Furniture upholstery has been refashioned with bold splattered paint and an old cable spool echoes the vintage clock above.

page 174: The legs of the side table were found in the street and are topped with a wooden pallet. Artistic touches such as the painting on the door can be found all over the apartment, adding to its bohemian feel.

see also page 6: The seating in the living room ranges from an original French Louis XV antique, which dates back to the 18th century, to a 21st-century Clay chair by Marteen Baas.

GARAGE LOFT

BRICKS STUDIO | AMSTERDAM, NETHERLANDS

Interior designer James Van der Velden was born in London and later moved with his family to an old manor house in the English countryside. When they relocated to the Netherlands, his mother created a beautiful family home, changing the interior twice a year for summer and winter. Growing up in such inspiring homes sparked Van der Velden's own creativity and passion for interior design. After studying spatial design in London and working for designers such as Kelly Hoppen Interiors and Piet Boon, he returned to Amsterdam in 2010 to set up his own practice, Bricks Studio.

Looking at the graffiti-covered roll-down door of the Garage Loft in Amsterdam from the street, passers-by are unable to guess what lies beyond. Amid a plethora of beautiful period buildings in the city, the humble facade of a 1950s commercial building was one of the things that appealed most to Van der Velden, who knew how he wanted to transform the space the moment he set eyes on it.

The brief was simply to convert the garage into an inspiring and liveable home. Originally it was a storage space that was later converted into a garage where cars were fixed. 'As it was an old garage in an old part of town, I wanted to create a space which felt as though it had been there for many years,' says Van der Velden. 'In all my projects, the first things I look at are the existing elements and features that I can reuse, such as old doors, old beams, beautiful old walls and even old wood behind plasterboard.'

The Garage Loft conversion took just one year to complete. Infused with Van der Velden's signature eclectic style, the decor blends materials, antiques and objects from a range of different eras, with a modern orientation. A key feature of the project is its floor-to-ceiling steel and glass walls. These were used to make the biggest structural change of the renovation: a glass atrium surrounding a courtyard in the centre of the living space. Exposed to the elements, the courtyard brings in fresh air and daylight while keeping the space very open. Beyond the garden, new walls were formed to house a guest bedroom and bathroom as well as a master bedroom that has a vintage motorcycle on display.

One of the reasons Van der Velden chose the garage was that it seemed the perfect backdrop for showcasing his personal collection of vintage and antique finds, mostly picked up at Parisian flea markets or via online auctions. His secret to blending the old and the new is creating contrast. 'Combining existing elements with the new can create an aesthetically pleasing space full of surprise,' he says. 'Working within spatial limitations can also be a good thing. There are set parameters, but this is an advantage. It makes you more creative.'

RENOVATE **INNOVATE**

PHOTOS

page 177: Drawn to the raw structure and design of the existing garage, Van der Velden aimed to create an industrial liveable space for his Garage Loft. The floor-to-ceiling steel and glass atrium brings in natural light and fresh air.

page 178, top: Van der Velden turned his home into a museum of curiosities with items he has collected over the years. The vintage sofa was bought at an online auction.

page 178, bottom: A few of the walls were left as they were found in order to maintain an industrial feel.

page 179, top: The front part of the garage continues to be used as a parking space, so it still looks like a garage from the street. Van der Velden designed the dining table himself. Large industrial pendant lighting hangs overhead.

page 179, bottom: The train station clock was a gift from Van der Velden's father and separates the kitchen from the living area.

page 180, top: The existing garage was one large open space, so walls were created to make two bedrooms and a bathroom. Black painted doorframes echo the lines of the steel and glass atrium, a theme that recurs in the bathroom tiling. A vintage motorcycle is on display in the master bedroom.

page 180, bottom: Wooden pallets were used for the guest bedroom furniture. A vintage map of 19th-century Germany stands out against a black-painted wall.

LA FABRICA

RICARDO BOFILL TALLER DE ARQUITECTURA | BARCELONA, SPAIN

In 1963, after graduating from the School of Architecture in Geneva, Ricardo Bofill gathered together an international team of architects, engineers, sociologists and philosophers to create what is today known as Ricardo Bofill Taller de Arquitectura. Since founding his firm, Bofill has won numerous awards and worked on over 1,000 projects in 40 countries. His prolific portfolio includes urban master plans, public infrastructure, airports, cultural buildings and offices as well as private houses, interiors, furniture and product design.

The headquarters for Bofill's studio can be regarded as one of the most impressive examples of adaptive reuse. A building of palatial proportions, La Fabrica is located in Sant Just Desvern on the outskirts of Barcelona and was, in its previous life, a cement factory dating back to the late 19th century. The complex is comprised of eight silos that house offices, a models laboratory, archives, a library, a projections room and a gigantic space known as the Cathedral, which is used for exhibitions, concerts and cultural events. The building also contains a private residence for Bofill and is surrounded by gardens.

'My first encounter with La Fabrica was in 1973,' says Bofill. 'I found enormous silos, a tall smokestack, four kilometres of underground tunnels, machine rooms in good shape, huge empty spaces filled nonetheless with magic. Seduced by the contradictions and the ambiguity of the place, I decided quickly to retain the factory and modify its original brutality, sculpting it like a work of art. I started with a very romantic idea to bring nature into this industrial place. I wanted to live there for the pleasure of the challenge. In architecture there are no lost causes. This is what I wanted to prove, by transforming the factory into my study and my house. Dealing with an existing structure involves an additional dilemma, which is what to preserve and what should be demolished. Finding the balance is always the greatest challenge. A sensitive juxtaposition proves that contemporary architectural interventions can enhance a building's historical value. I wanted to prove that everything could be extracted from an existing space: an industrial building that might seem limiting; the implementation of two different programmes that are apparently incompatible (the professional activity of my practice, study and team meetings, and my own private daily life). Today, they coexist perfectly. It is the only place where I can concentrate and come up with ideas in the most abstract manner.'

At La Fabrica, Surrealist elements can be found at every turn. As Bofill explains, 'paradoxical stairs' lead to nowhere and spaces of strange proportions have no obvious function. 'They are magical because of their tension and disproportion,' he posits. 'This project is evidence of the fact that an imaginative architect may adapt any space to a new function, no matter how different it may be from the original one.'

RENOVATE **INNOVATE**

PHOTOS

page 183: The construction work for converting the factory began with partial destruction of the site with dynamite and jackhammers, a process which lasted for more than a year and a half. La Fabrica's Cathedral space has a ceiling height of 10 metres.

page 184: The upper living-room interior is furnished with long white drapes. Elements of historical Catalan architecture can be seen in the elongated arched windows, reminiscent of Barcelona's Gothic Quarter. All the furniture is made by Bofill's design department.

page 185: The Cathedral part of La Fabrica is used for exhibitions and cultural events.

pages 186–7: The entire complex was planted with lush gardens containing eucalyptus, palms, mimosa trees and cypresses. With plants climbing the walls and hanging from the roof, the building becomes a peaceful oasis in an industrial setting.

page 188: The factory also houses Bofill's private residence and guest accommodation, including eight bedrooms and twelve bathrooms.

see also page 4 and pages 158–9.

TRIBECA LOFT

ANDREW FRANZ ARCHITECT | NEW YORK, UNITED STATES

The award-winning Tribeca Loft sits at the top of a six-storey Neo-Romanesque building in Manhattan, built between 1884 and 1885 and designed by architect George W. DaCunha. The structure originally served as a warehouse for a variety of businesses, including the Harrel Soap Company, a wrought iron pipes and fittings manufacturer, a metal spinning company and several grocers and purveyors. The top-floor residence was originally occupied by the Romanoff Caviar Company and was used as a refrigeration area. In more recent years, it housed a studio space for an artist and stylist before being purchased by architect Andrew Franz's clients.

The clients were looking to create a three-bedroom home with large entertaining areas, outdoor space and an authentic loft character. When Franz discovered the 3,000-square-foot space, it was almost raw, with concrete floors, practically no interior walls, poor air circulation and little natural light, despite its high ceiling. 'A mezzanine was located below the ceiling's lowest point and you had to duck in order to navigate it,' says Franz. 'However, the historic character and dynamic conditions of the space were striking and incredibly inspiring. Our design reconfigures the space as a warm, light-filled and transparent residence imbued with intermingling natural, urban and historic elements. Despite the large commercial scale, we wanted the space to be welcoming.'

Franz transformed the space by reorienting the mezzanine from its original location along the west wall to the south wall, where the ceiling height is greater. The new level features a sunken interior glass court with a retractable glass roof that opens up to a green terrace above. 'Not only does the interior court bring in light, views and air, the new sense of height with multiple, overlapping levels of occupancy are thrilling,' he says. 'The experience and views completely change depending on where you are in the building.'

Reclaimed materials from the loft and from outside sources were used alongside locally sourced modern materials, creating a visual discourse between old and new. 'We originally anticipated a lighter, warmer colour for the beams and columns, but when they started removing the paint, we discovered deeply blackened, charred surfaces,' recalls Franz. 'We spent weeks trying to remedy this before realizing we had to embrace the condition. In hindsight, it was an obvious and fortuitous decision. The rich, charred colour is warmer and creates an ombre effect rising from the floor to the ceiling. The members are bent and twisted from the fire, almost resembling tree trunks. The effect softens their impact and the geometry of the space. Sometimes your obstacles become your best assets. The best designs are considerate of their environment and timeless, neither bold statements of today nor recreations of the past. The beauty of working with existing buildings is that they often have stories to tell or stories waiting to be uncovered.'

PHOTOS

page 191: The interior court with retractable glass roof adds accessible outdoor space and views to the Tribeca Loft while also bringing natural light into the primary living zones.

pages 192–3: The original charred beams and columns reveal the building's industrial history as a caviar warehouse. Treads and landings for the custom steel staircase are made from repurposed timbers from the old roof joists. A former elevator winch from the building was converted into a custom 7-foot-long coffee table with reclaimed wood pivoting elements.

page 194, top: Originally the loft had no access to the roof. By reorienting the existing mezzanine to the south wall where the ceiling height is greater, there was enough height to create the interior courtyard, which also provided the best access point to the new roof terrace.

page 194, bottom: The residence is unified by a walnut fascia, which runs throughout the building.

page 195, top: In order to bring light deep into the loft, Franz created transparency throughout the length of the apartment, with glass partitions instead of solid walls at the north end, where the bedrooms are located.

page 195, bottom left: Franz wanted to create a calm oasis in the urban jungle by incorporating nature as much as possible. Reclaimed bluestone pavers were used on the rooftop terrace and a green roof garden contains native plant species that require little water.

page 195, bottom right: The apartment is furnished with mid-century antique furniture.

CARLTON NORTH
APARTMENT

HEARTH | MELBOURNE, AUSTRALIA

Sarah Trotter originally studied architecture in Queensland and Melbourne. While working for Australian architecture practices including Six Degrees, Peter Elliott and Robert Simeoni, she pursued independent creative endeavours ranging from art direction for film to food styling. In 2012, she founded interior architecture and design practice Hearth. She is also the founder of product design studio Groupwork and one half of the food website Trotski & Ash.

Located next to the client's mid-century childhood home, Carlton North Apartment was once an original 1970s Merchant Builders garage. Founded by David Yencken and John Ridge, Merchant Builders Pty Ltd was a highly influential project house-building firm that erected modernist homes in Australia from the 1960s to the 1990s.

'The project initially started by looking at a proposal for a garage conversion,' says Trotter. 'It had original rendered brick walls and heavy, exposed Oregon timber roof beams which informed the zones of the internal configuration. Myself and the client, Alex Kennedy, worked together to make the space as functional as possible within the limited space, taking into consideration the light and borrowed views to the garden. The amenity is really what makes this project special: views to the trees upon waking and visibility through the spaces.'

The existing structure happened to prove perfect for creating a habitable space. Trotter adds, 'It was wide enough to accommodate the need for circulation and the various spaces needed to make a home. The ramp up, which was the original ramping for the car space, was great for allowing plumbing to the WC at the rear. The ramp was then covered and evened out to create the bed platform. The overhead ceiling beams also delineated three zones for sleeping, eating and resting.'

Much of the apartment is made from reclaimed materials. All of the lighting and bathroom fittings were sourced from auction houses, online sales and junkyards. Trotter and the client decided that, because they had time to invest, they could source quality fittings at better prices as opposed to new, lesser-quality fixtures. They ultimately repurposed timber from the building and used it as bench tops, and the client worked hard to find all of the taps for the bath, sinks and even the toilet second-hand. The island bench is the original workbench from the existing garage.

'All of my work is a response to the existing conditions of a site,' Trotter says. 'I love the way that working within an existing shell can create new ideas, push boundaries and present new and surprising opportunities for views and relationships between spaces. It is challenging and with that comes reward. I think urban renewal and repurposing structures and objects will be essential for the future. Too often the reuse of buildings is imposed by regulation or heritage recommendation rather than being embraced. I believe we need to have more ingenuity and use all of the resources we have at hand, without waste, to create a better built environment.'

RENOVATE **INNOVATE**

PHOTOS

page 199: The vintage mid-century daybed at Carlton North Apartment is used as a couch. The Boucherouite rug was bought at online auction and adds a splash of colour to the space. The artwork is a photograph by Conor O'Brien.

page 200, top left: A platform defines the sleeping zone. It also has a highlight window that looks out onto the trees and the laneway, letting in morning light while allowing privacy.

page 200, top right: The original apartment featured bagged brickwork and Oregon beams. These were infilled with whitewashed plywood to form the ceiling. The bathing area and WC are separated by a two-way bathroom bench containing a reclaimed sink.

page 200, bottom: Bench tops are refinished timber salvaged from the existing garage. Japanese tiles form a splashback in the kitchen.

page 201: The kitchen features bulkhead lighting and handmade leather door handles on the cabinetry. The island is the workbench from the building's previous life as a garage. Shelves are adorned with Marloe Morgan ceramics and the sink and taps are reclaimed from a science lab.

page 202: The clawfoot bath was found at a reclaimed furniture yard and the mirror at an online auction. Indoor plants add to the sense of calm.

THE CHAPEL

Architect Stefan Camenzind is the founder of Evolution Design, an award-winning architecture and design studio based in Zurich. It was while exploring Teesdale, a walking district in the beautiful North Pennines, that Camenzind and his brother-in-law came across the Ebenezer Methodist Chapel. Built in 1880, it served the local community for 107 years before closing in 1987. The chapel was found boarded up, vacant and in a poor state of disrepair. Captivated by the raw beauty of the landscape and the open horizon, they decided to take on the derelict building and, by 2015, it was transformed into a unique holiday home for seven guests.

'We thought this would be such a fantastic place for our families to come to,' explains Camenzind. 'The location of the chapel on the top of a hill, within such an amazing landscape, is so stunning and memorable that it becomes obvious why it was built in this location. People used to come here for contemplation and celebration, for beautiful occasions such as baptisms and weddings. The chapel has a very special positive spirit and this was the feeling that we wanted to retain.'

The harsh weather conditions of Upper Teesdale meant the chapel, in its exposed location, had suffered years of strong winds and driving rain. Because it had not been sufficiently maintained, a lot was required to make the building habitable. In addition to considerable water ingress and damage to the interior finishes, the roof had deteriorated and the rafters needed replacing. There were also no services, which meant water, electricity and sewage treatment had to be newly installed.

Camenzind's aim for reconstructing the chapel was to preserve the historic building's fabric and bring its unique structure back to life by retaining the grandness of the original hall, as well as the beautiful Gothic windows that flood the space with daylight. Locating master bedrooms on the mezzanine floor above the original window line was a challenge, as it gave limited headroom upstairs. This meant the team had to look for smart solutions for making the bedrooms feel more spacious, practical and comfortable for guests. 'Every detail, including the built-in wardrobes, had to be thought through,' Camenzind relates. 'We even built a 1:1 mock-up in our office to test the layout and ensure it worked at full scale. We wanted visitors to be able to appreciate the history and local architecture while providing a beautiful environment to explore the countryside and its vast range of activities. Historic buildings like the chapel have the charm of ageing and growing together with their surroundings, a natural quality that cannot be replicated.'

PHOTOS

page 205: Camenzind preserved the historic stonework of the chapel and recycled the roof tiles, which ensured they would fit well into the existing landscape.

page 206, top: Before the chapel was built in 1880, the local community had shared another chapel with the Baptists until they decided to build their own. Local men quarried the stone, and women held a bazaar to raise funds. In total, the building costs came to £350.

page 206, bottom: The chapel is located in the walking district of Teesdale in the North Pennines, close to the famous High Force Waterfall.

page 207, top: The interior is modern, open and bright with traditional details that complement the building's location and history. The kitchen dining table is made out of reclaimed wood collected from an abandoned railway station. Reclaimed timber railway sleepers were also used as steps, leading from the terrace to the garden.

page 207, bottom left: Stairs lead up to the mezzanine floor, which contains three bedrooms and two en suite bathrooms. There is also a fourth bedroom and family bathroom on the ground floor.

page 207, bottom right: The chapel is now a cosy self-catering cottage for up to seven guests, offering stunning views of the Dales. A homely rural feel is maintained throughout.

THE WHITE ROOM

LYNDA GARDENER | MELBOURNE, AUSTRALIA

For the last 25 years, Melbourne-based interior designer, stylist and retailer Lynda Gardener has resided in the trendy area of Fitzroy, a creative hub renowned for its fashion, art, cafés and boutiques. Gardener started working in fashion for a large company at the age of 19 and quickly worked her way up, specializing in visual merchandising and purchasing props for the company's stores around Australia. After around 10 years she decided to go it alone and open up her own store. Her shop, Lynda Gardener: CURATED, sells homeware, vintage furniture, rustic one-off finds and pieces from her personal collection.

The White Room is a studio apartment located in what was originally a warehouse for a mattress factory, built in the early 1900s. Gardener purchased the building when it was derelict and contained nothing but abandoned cars. After an extensive renovation that involved dealing with a caved-in ceiling and an asbestos issue, she has been living there for over 15 years.

The studio is situated in an area that once contained the bathrooms and washrooms for the factory's staff; Gardener had originally turned it into an office. 'It was a lovely bright room to which I added old French doors found at a salvage yard and a small shower/bathroom, but over the years it wasn't really used enough,' she explains. 'I already owned a couple of rental accommodation properties, so I came up with the idea to turn this special place, which already had its own entrance, into a bespoke studio space. I pulled everything out and started from scratch. I sourced gorgeous old furniture and wanted a unique cosy monochrome fit-out that would be completely different to any standard hotel room.'

Gardener has an expert eye for vintage finds and has carefully curated the space with a mix of industrial lighting, handmade French linen and thrifted artwork. Everything in the room is vintage except for the bedding, rug and bed. She says, 'I have been a collector all my life and am a little spontaneous with it. I've bought and sold from places all over the world and am forever travelling to different flea markets, rummaging for the next find.'

Usually, Gardener begins interiors projects by adding a fresh coat of paint to the walls. 'The old, found furniture pieces always stand out against a crisp background,' she says. 'I think old with a little new is the perfect mix in any room. I might contrast period features with a new over-dyed rug or a piece of contemporary artwork, for example. Nothing can compare to working with an old space. Age and use create character, and the crooked floors and walls, cracks and old finishes are all the things that make it instantly unique. Nothing is predictable and that's what I love the most. I also can't imagine a time where "old finds" would not be used in design, particularly in my world. Decorating with collected old pieces reveals your personality and makes a space your own.'

REIMAGINED

PHOTOS

page 211: The White Room's kitchen trolley with stainless steel top was once a dental bench, sourced from a second-hand store in the countryside. The white glass door dental cabinet, now used for kitchenware, was found in Melbourne many years ago. Externally the wall is covered in Boston ivy, which managed to make its way into the studio – Gardener loved the look of it so much she decided to keep it there.

page 212–13: A factory stool is used as a bedside table and the white-painted 1920s country table was another flea market find.

page 214: The self-contained room, which is rented out as a holiday let, has its own kitchen, en suite bathroom and separate entrance. Taps and sinks were found at local salvage yards.

see also page 250: To complete the monochrome look in The White Room, Gardener hunted for black-and-white etchings and pictures. It was also the perfect space to display a large work of art depicting an old man's face, brought back from Istanbul.

KENT RESERVOIR

BRINKWORTH | KENT, UNITED KINGDOM

Brinkworth CEO Kevin Brennan first discovered these disused reservoirs in Kent in 2007, with planning permission already granted for conversion into two single-family dwellings. The East Reservoir was built in 1955 alongside an earlier structure that was built in 1938 by the architect Shane Jell. On a hill above the Kent village of Harrietsham, the identical structures sat over a natural aquifer, providing 500,000 gallons of fresh water to the surrounding area. In the 1980s, Mid Kent Water made them redundant.

Brinkworth had previously worked on successive alterations to the London home of Young British Artist Dinos Chapman and textile designer Tiphaine de Lussy. As they had been searching for a countryside residence, Brennan knew that the Kent Reservoir project would be of interest to them. It had ample space for guest accommodation, a studio, gallery space and extensive recreational areas, including a swimming pool, sauna, terraces and gardens.

Inspired by the writings of his professor and mentor Fred Scott, author of *On Altering Architecture*, Brennan says, 'At Brinkworth we believe that interior design is largely defined by the relationship with the host building. The host, in this instance, was not a piece of architecture, but a hidden industrial relic, an engineered space, and its permission to alter it was limited.'

The biggest challenge was maintaining the stability of the building during the alterations. 'Initially, the approach was more akin to contemporary archaeology and engineering, as the preservation of the structure was fundamental and the raison d'être of the project,' Brennan explains. 'This, combined with the richness and quality of the concrete surface, effected by decades of holding millions of gallons of water, would dictate the overall aesthetic and the design needed to be subservient to it. Sustainability and the need to retain the reservoir were also high on our agenda.' The programme of works included ground source heat pumps, rainwater harvesting, heat recovery systems and restoration of the local ecology.

Brinkworth created six rooms on the ground floor within the concrete grid, which was made up of five-metre-square bays, evenly spaced with pillars. The internal walls also provided support to the existing structure. Other alterations included incisions made in the shell to allow daylight into the interior, as well as a 30 × 5 metre slot that formed a south-facing courtyard. The structure was topped with a modernist-inspired glass pavilion.

'Commerce and economic factors have meant our industrial heritage is going through architectural upcycling,' says Brennan. 'The refurbishment of redundant factories and public houses, from Tate Modern to our warehouse stock, have all influenced this project in one way or another. The ability to rehabilitate these structures and breathe new life into them adds new value and becomes a moment in the historical continuum.'

RENOVATE **INNOVATE**

PHOTOS

page 217: The arrangement of the rooms at Kent Reservoir was dictated by the concrete grid of the existing structure. Six rooms were created on the ground floor with polished concrete flooring, including the open-plan kitchen.

page 218, top: The house has been built with sustainability and ecology in mind. The surrounding landscape conceals a rainwater and wastewater discharge and harvesting plant. This treats the water and enables it to be circulated through the home for flushing the toilets and irrigating the garden areas.

page 218, bottom: Two large, en suite double bedrooms, a master bedroom suite and two guest bedrooms all have direct access to a lap pool situated on the south sub-terrace.

page 219, top: The bedrooms are furnished with soft textured fabrics and elegant chandeliers, contrasting with the hard, cool concrete that was left exposed throughout.

page 219, bottom: A glass pavilion was added to the top of the structure, which opens out onto a roof terrace. Warm oak flooring was used in the upper parts of the house.

pages 220–21: The kitchen and living area on the ground floor has a 15-metre collapsible patio window. This extends the space out to the garden.

page 222: Ground source heat pumps, concealed beneath a nearby meadow, recover natural heat from the ground and provide warm water to the underfloor heating system and swimming pool.

LE MOULIN ET LE FOUR

PIET HEIN EEK | MAVALEIX, FRANCE

After graduating from the Design Academy Eindhoven, Piet Hein Eek started his company with the aim of creating products where the full processes of design, production, distribution and sales would all be taken care of. He now works from a 10,000-square-metre building in Eindhoven, where workshops for wood, steel, upholstery, assembly, spraying and ceramics are all brought together under one roof. The furniture and objects he produces are either limited edition or made in short series, often from seemingly worthless or waste materials.

Situated in the Dordogne region of France, the 19th-century former mill and outbuildings of Le Moulin et Le Four were discovered as a crumbling ruin. With the project on hold for five years, Eek's renovation was a labour of love lasting 10 years in total. In collaboration with architect Iggie Dekkers, the site has now been transformed into two dwellings that are rented out as holiday accommodation.

Eek's work has always been inspired by making the best of what's already there, which explains his fascination for ruins. He says, 'I think it's because a ruin is suggestive of the past but, at the same time, offers the possibility to reconstruct it, so it also contains the future. Since working on Le Moulin, I have described my work as finding the most logical and pragmatic way to connect the past with the future. By working on this project for so long, I came to understand more about the location and how people lived and worked back then. This consciousness of the past and respect for what is already there is echoed in the reason why the mill was built here in the first place. Because of what nature provided: the water creates the power, the valley provides volume, and stones from the rocks along the stream construct the buildings and dyke, which is also formed by the narrowness of the valley.'

Much of the wood used in the renovation was sourced from the surrounding forest and used for the roofs and windows. Inspired by the rotting wood that was rescued from the ruin, Eek used some of the old panels to make sofas, which now furnish the mill interior. To ensure the new roof resembled its original, it is made from wood salvaged from a military building in Belgium. The most significant reused material, however, is the stones from the existing ruin – these were dug up with machines and each one was individually selected to rebuild exposed walls in the traditional style.

For Eek, reusing materials is simply the most obvious thing to do. But, he says, 'Rather than trying to find solutions to bad consumption habits, I believe common sense should ultimately lead us to consume and live with less. We seem to think that everything is available for us. In any creative process, it might be good to consider that the world does not by its nature provide what one wishes, but we should use what the world actually offers.'

RENOVATE **INNOVATE**

PHOTOS

page 225: The rooms in Le Moulin are filled with artworks and furniture pieces by Eek and other artists. The colourful striped wall painting is by Jan van de Ploeg. The living room also contains Eek's Old Lampshade Lamp, a spherical chandelier comprised of 62 vintage lights.

page 226, top: The bright orange Beam Cabinet is made from old beams. The sofas are made from old rotten oak panels that Eek rescued from the ruins of the mill.

page 226, bottom left: Salvaged stones were placed on top of each other, one by one, like a puzzle. Cement was used instead of the mud and soil that would have been employed in ancient times.

page 226, bottom right: Eek's Line Lamps hang in the rafters of one of the bedrooms and are made from mirrored stainless steel.

page 227, top: The mill's cluster of buildings have been renovated into two homes called Le Moulin and Le Four and can be rented out by two families or one large group. A 20-metre-long canal is also available for swimming in during the summer months.

page 227, bottom left: The outside terrace of the upper house features a limited-edition piece by Eek called Tubes Chair, made from reclaimed pipes.

page 227, bottom right: The Old Windows Cabinet was specifically designed for this space to draw attention to the height of the room. It was made transparent so that the wall can be seen behind it.

page 228: A chandelier made from plywood creates a focal point over a cosy living room in Le Four.

FITZROY LOFT

ARCHITECTS EAT | MELBOURNE, AUSTRALIA

MacRobertson's Steam Confectionery Works was a chocolate factory founded by Sir Macpherson Robertson in 1880. The company's premises were based at their factory in Fitzroy, Australia, for 100 years before moving to Ringwood, Victoria. The building was then adapted for residential use, as an office, and even as an Aikido dojo in the early 1990s. In 2015, Melbourne-based firm Architects EAT were given the task of creating a light-filled 250-square-metre apartment, which occupies the first floor of the brick warehouse.

The factory and warehouse complex was built between 1890 and 1910 and, in heritage terms, is considered aesthetically and historically significant to the City of Yarra – this means that any alterations to the appearance of the building visible from public view are not permitted. Architect Albert Mo says, 'Keeping up the integrity of the original factory bones was vital. We tore down the walls and floors that were built in more recent years to expose charred beams and remnant paint, the scars of its past. These were left untouched.'

The local council had advised against unroofed or open upper-level decks, so the main challenge was finding a way to bring light and air into the building. The chosen design was based around a series of spaces linked by three internal voids. The first void is a courtyard connected to the main living room and kitchen, creating an 'Aussie backyard'. The roof was removed to create an open-air garden and replaced with a fine galvanized expanded mesh. This was done to minimize disruption to the facade of the building and maintain consistency. The second void separates the private zones from the living areas, and upper spaces are linked by a suspended steel bridge. A third void was created in the library, allowing soft southern ambient light to filter in. The three voids preserve the sense of height from the original factory while also creating an airy, light-filled space.

Steel structure and windows are used throughout, providing a visual contrast to the original timber. Unlike other warehouse conversions, the team decided not to furnish the space with 'warehouse feel' elements such as industrial lighting and metro tiles. 'We instead injected modern comfort and adequacy into a vintage shell,' Mo says. 'By embracing the constraints of the four bounding walls of the old factory and its sawtooth roofs, this project exemplifies what can be achieved by careful orchestration of spaces, manipulation of light and choreography of materials. The texture, history, tactility and even smell have enriched the meaning of the space that we have created. Like many, I find it inspirational to see how one can creatively use building materials, whether they're salvaged, found or donated, to solve problems while keeping costs low and designs courageous. If we cannot find a way to reuse our existing building stock, there is no point in even talking about a sustainable future. This kind of architecture and design will only continue and expand, generation after generation, out of both necessity and curiosity.'

PHOTOS

page 231: A courtyard at the Fitzroy Loft was created by replacing part of the roof with a fine mesh, transforming the old chocolate factory into a light-filled modern family home. The 250-square-metre apartment occupies the first floor of the brick warehouse, with an entry door at street level. The project won the 2016 Australian Interior Design Award for Residential Design.

page 232: A bridge is located in one of the floor-to-ceiling voids, allowing movement to and from the upstairs rooms. The bridge has a perforated floor to create a sense of lightness. Louvre windows were placed at the top of the sawtooth roof, allowing hot air to escape in summer months by way of cross-ventilation.

page 233, top: The third void lets light into the library area and mezzanine study above. It also displays the original timber column and beam.

page 233, bottom, and page 234, top: Steel window frames surrounding the courtyard allow plenty of light to flow into the rooms.

page 234, bottom: The interior was furnished to reflect modern living, without opting for typical warehouse-style detailing. Rays of light penetrate from above, creating a play of shadows on the white polished concrete floor.

PAVILION D'ÉTÉ

NOÉMIE MENEY | TOULON, FRANCE

The history of the brick shack that stood neglected in the garden of a 1930s holiday home in Toulon, France, near Marseille, was somewhat a mystery. The original high-ceilinged building, however, had a remarkable relationship with the area around it because of an ample arch, so the owners asked architect Noémie Meney to covert it into self-contained guest quarters. Her aim was to retain its sense of roominess and, in particular, its seamlessness with the outdoors.

Inspiration for the interior of the pavilion was taken from the phenomena of a swallow's nest clinging to an attic's framework. The 'nest' occupies the upper volume of the shed, hidden from view by wickerwork screens. Like Venetian blinds or moucharabieh (latticework windows frequently found in Islamic architecture), they allow a person to see out without being seen. Meney explains, 'Wickerwork offers a very good quality of luminosity and a soothing colour of light that cannot be achieved with a cold material such as metal.'

The ground floor contains the living room, with the kitchen and bathroom partitioned off. The shower area has a large curtain for privacy, but can also be used open. 'One can have a shower in a vast open space, while enjoying a view of the natural environment. Thus the exceptional rapport between the inside and outside of the shelter is preserved,' says Meney.

The biggest challenge was not only to conserve the pavilion's link to the outdoors but to retain its inside height as well as the arch, which allows you to see the garden and sky from anywhere in the building. The solution was to separate the new facade from the old one. The new facade is set back inside, so that the new building occupies just half of the volume of the old building.

Meney also decided to omit a front door. Instead, a folding door was placed in line with the wicker screen, so that only the back half of the building closes. 'I decided not to break the arch with new elements,' she explains. 'In my opinion, closing the arch with a door would have put a physical limitation between inside and outside, which would have contradicted my intentions for the project. I chose wicker for the screen because I wanted a living material, with its own imperfections and irregularities. This material is not static, the colour changes and it moves a little with the humidity. In my aim to create closeness with nature, I liked the idea that not everything in the universe can be controlled by humans. I didn't want something fixed that never changes. Moreover, it was a way to make a link with the old building, which is built from materials that are close to 100 years old. The wicker makes reference to handicraft and heritage in a contemporary way. I think architecture should never be imposed as an object but, on the contrary, reveal the place, highlight it and underline its characteristics.'

page 237: The guesthouse is designed to be fully equipped for a couple, featuring a kitchen, bathroom, bedroom and sitting room.

page 238: To ensure the sense of space in the building was not lost, only the back half of the structure was converted into living quarters, with the large arch left untouched. Wickerwork, a material traditionally used to make chairs, is here given a modern spin.

page 239, top: The 'nest' part of the living space takes up as little volume as possible and is hidden from view behind wickerwork screens.

page 239, bottom left: The guest quarters can be closed off when required.

page 239, bottom right: Prior to being converted it was years since the building had been used, but it may have served as a garden atelier.

page 240: Wicker gives the space a warm glow when illuminated by night. The shower area on the ground floor can be used open, maintaining a link with the outdoors.

THE BERLIN LOFT

PHILIPP GERTNER | BERLIN, GERMANY

Polish-born Philipp Gertner moved to Germany with his family at the age of nine. After studying international business administration in Germany, Paris, New York and Argentina, he worked as an independent business coach for start-ups, with a focus on marketing. He then co-founded Fabrik 23 in 2014, a unique event location in the same factory as his apartment, The Berlin Loft. Since then, Gertner has mainly been focused on interior and furniture design.

The factory is over 100 years old, hidden in a typical Berlin backyard of the city's old working-class quarter, Wedding. Built in 1906, it was originally home to numerous manufacturing businesses and workshops. Pocked with bullet holes, it still holds its scars from the Second World War. After the fall of the Berlin Wall the building was mostly empty, although it was frequently used for illegal parties with up to 1,000 guests. Today, the factory belongs to a wealthy New Yorker with a passion for the arts and is inhabited by numerous artists and craftspeople.

When Gertner first discovered the loft space in 2011 it hadn't been used for many years and was completely run down, with no electricity, running water or heating. The raw ceilings and walls, however, presented a perfect stage for rough, upcycled furniture and unique finds. 'The existing components of interiors and objects and the magic of patina are the basis for my work,' he says. 'My goal was to create rough beauty and elegance through the process of upcycling, combining vintage and industrial furniture with materials such as waste wood, copper, concrete or Corten steel. Over time, the qualities of reclaimed materials change in colour and appearance. They are also not subject to ever-changing trends and are imbued with history. I will never get bored of looking at the old drawing table, which was sourced from an architect's office. I use it as a bar and have equipped it with LEDs to illuminate my liquor bottles from underneath. It is so timeless.'

The flooring of Gertner's apartment is made from old pallet wood. The rooms are full of hand-built upcycled furniture that he has made from salvaged wood, vintage windows and doors, wine boxes, and bits and pieces found in the factory's basement. He has also built up a good network of dealers in Germany and Poland who can provide him with rare vintage finds. 'Old things not only have a personal story but change your attitude towards materialistic things,' he says. 'Production of new things has a negative impact but, with reclaimed products, suddenly consumption becomes ecological and fun. Not long ago, upcycling might have been viewed as a DIY thing with inferior quality and materials, but this is clearly changing as people recognize that it can be just the opposite.'

RENOVATE **INNOVATE**

page 243: The floor of Gertner's Berlin Loft is made from planks constructed out of recovered wood pallets.

page 244, top: Gertner's grandmother bought the side cabinet in Poland in the 1960s.

page 244, bottom: The dining table is made from waste wood and old pallets found in the factory's basement. The sideboard is made from old construction planks.

page 245, top left: A kitchen counter made from waste wood and pallet wood is paired with some old goldsmith's workshop stools. An old German factory lamp hangs overhead.

page 245, top right: Gertner salvaged the door to the oven in the basement, which used to heat the factory. He used it to craft a wardrobe that is also lined with a vertical garden made from recycled pallets. The small table was made from an old window and parquet flooring salvaged from the gym of a girls' school.

page 245, bottom: A storage unit is made from old French wine cases and recycled coffee bags. The kitchen fronts are made of waste wood and pallet wood with porcelain fuses found in the loft made into door handles.

pages 246–7: The sideboard is made of waste wood and a pair of small 19th-century windows found on eBay. The long shelf above the sideboard is made from a 100-year-old heavy cast iron ladder with a glass top, and the hanging lamp above is made from old pipes. On the left are two 1920s entrance doors salvaged from a villa in Berlin. The table is also made from old wine cases, waste wood and old pipes.

pages 248: The wooden locker was sourced from a Berlin factory and the unusual double-armed lamp above the locker was originally used to light two desks.

see also page 9.

DIRECTORY

RECLAIMED

Atlanta Treehouse
peterbahouth.com

Whitehorse
designbuildbluff.org

747 Wing House
davidhertzfaia.com

Saigon House
a21studio.com.vn

Remisenpavillon
wirth-architekten.com

The Love Art Studio
facebook.com/TheLoveArtStudio

Cañon City Container Cabin
tomecekstudio.com

Telegraph Pole House
whbca.com

Hut on Stilts
nozomi-nakabayashi.com

Tiny Texas Houses
tinytexashouses.com

El Mirador House
ccarquitectos.com.mx

The HemLoft
thehemloft.com

REVIVED

York House Apartment
patricklewisarchitects.com

The White House
wtarchitecture.com

Tiny House
jhinteriordesign.com

Milanese Apartment
thechicfish.com

Astley Castle
wwmarchitects.co.uk

Eixample Apartment
eoarquitectura.com

Russell-Fontanez Apartment
lot-ek.com

Home B
quintanapartners.com

Berlin Summer Apartment
loft-kolasinski.com

REIMAGINED

Alpine Barn Apartment
ofis-a.si

Light Studio
manoloyllera.com

Garage Loft
bricksstudio.nl

La Fabrica
ricardobofill.com

Tribeca Loft
andrewfranz.com

Carlton North Apartment
hearthstudio.com.au

The Chapel
evolution-design.info

The White Room
thewhitehousedaylesford.com.au

Kent Reservoir
brinkworth.co.uk

Le Moulin et Le Four
pietheineek.nl

Fitzroy Loft
eatas.com.au

Pavilion d'Été
meney_noemie@yahoo.fr

The Berlin Loft
the-berlin-loft.com

PICTURE CREDITS

ACKNOWLEDGEMENTS

A huge thank you to all the architects, designers, artists, makers and photographers who contributed to this book.

Special thanks go to Ali Gitlow, Andrew Hansen, Martha Jay, Paul Sloman and Prestel Publishing.

Thanks also to Jacqueline Milborrow, David Milborrow, Georgios Kopanias, Alexandros Nikolaidis and Elizabeth Simpson for all your encouragement and support.

This book is dedicated to John Brooke Edwards.

© Prestel Verlag, Munich · London · New York, 2017
A member of Verlagsgruppe Random House GmbH
Neumarkter Strasse 28 · 81673 Munich

Prestel Publishing Ltd.
14-17 Wells Street
London W1T 3PD

Prestel Publishing
900 Broadway, Suite 603
New York, NY 10003

Library of Congress Control Number: 2016954060

A CIP catalogue record for this book is available from the British Library.

Editorial direction: Ali Gitlow
Copyediting and proofreading: Martha Jay
Design and layout: Paul Sloman | +SUBTRACT
Production management: Friederike Schirge

Separations: Ludwig Media

Printing and binding: DZS

Paper: Profisilk

Verlagsgruppe Random House FSC® N001967

Printed in Slovenia

ISBN 978-3-7913-8309-5

www.prestel.com

MIX
Paper from
responsible sources
FSC® C112556
FSC
www.fsc.org